Daniel:
Made Easy for the Layman

Harold F. Hunter, Th.D.

Trinity Academic Press

Trinity Academic Press

World Wide Web: Trinitysem.edu
Email:Contact@trinitysem.edu

©1985 by Harold F. Hunter. Edited for 2015 publication by Braxton Hunter

All rights reserved. No part of this publication may be reproduced, stored in a retrieval system, or transmitted in any form or by any means – electronic, mechanical, photocopy, recording, or any other – except for brief quotations in printed reviews, without the prior permission of the author.

All Scripture quotations taken from the King James Version of the Bible.

ISBN-13: 978-0692566411 (Trinity Academic Press)
ISBN-10: 0692566414

Printed in the United States of America

To Helen James and her daughter, Cindy, of Etowah, Tennessee, who have found their defense of the faith an arduous task, but one that has brought them an immeasurable love and appreciation for the absolute inerrancy of God': Word, and, in so doing, have warmed my heart with the ever-present remembrances of their daily walk with Christ as two of God's choicest servants.

Table of Contents

MAN WITH A PURPOSE	1
THE DREAM OF A KING	15
THE FIERY FURNACE	29
NEBUCHADNEZZAR'S TREE-VISION	41
HANDWRITING ON THE WALL	57
DANIEL IN THE DEN OF LIONS	69
PROPHECIES OF WORLD EMPIRES	83
THE INFLUENCE OF ALEXANDER THE GREAT	99
THE SEVENTY WEEKS OF DANIEL	113
HELP FOR THE MOURNING	127
ANTIOCHUS AND ANTICHRIST	141
THE TWO RESURRECTIONS	159

Chapter One

Man With A Purpose

The Book of Daniel stands as a written work of monumental importance in the Old Testament. It is a composite of instructional passages, prophecies, human interest stories, and personal challenges. Each page is filled with words of wisdom that are presented in the poignant style of a man whose heart was fixed on God.

The liberal Bible professor says that it is beyond human reason and belief to accept Daniel as the author of this book that bears his name. This assertion is based on the fact of detailed prophetic statements made in the book. No mortal man, the liberal suggests, could have possibly foreseen these events. Therefore, the book must have been the product of someone living after the events discussed in the Book of Daniel had occurred. Of course, such liberals have difficulty in simply trusting God's Word in matters that cut across the grain of their own ludicrous interpretations.

The one sure way of determining the authorship of the book is to consider the position of Jesus concerning it. What does He say'! In Matthew 24:15 are these words of our Lord:

"When ye, therefore, shall see the abomination of desolation spoken of by Daniel the prophet, stand in the holy place. . . "

Please note that Jesus identifies Daniel by the title, "the prophet." That firmly establishes two points. First, Daniel was the human author of the book, not some impostor who lived two hundred years later. Second, he lived before the times of the prophecies and was, as a result, designated as a prophet. Do not be shaken by the silly babblings of those who deny the trustworthiness of the Scriptures; the Bible is God's Word to man!

As we move through this study, an underlying theme will be frequently evident. We will be painfully aware of the chastisement of God's people as they suffer in judgment for the sins they committed in the land of Israel. For 490 years the

Jews had lived in the land of promise after their release from bondage in Egypt. Unprecedented prosperity had been theirs to enjoy.

But an awful cycle of sin appeared and became an habitual pattern of behavior in the nation's life. The Israelites seemed unable to break the grip of that deadly spiritual paralysis. This repetitive sin cycle began with God's gracious and bountiful blessings upon them, which resulted in their sinful disobedience, which resulted in God's chastisement of them, which resulted in their repentance, which resulted in God's forgiveness. Then, for a period of time, God would again pour out His blessings upon the nation and the cycle would begin again:

(1) Blessings;
(2) Sin;
(3) Chastisement;
(4) Forgiveness.

The Book of Daniel is a record of God's use of the pagan Babylonians as His divine chastening rod in the exercise of His punishment upon the nation of Israel. The children of Israel were assigned 70 years in exile from their homeland. Each day in the splendor of Babylon was a reminder of their golden years under Solomon. The temples erected to the false gods were but arrows of pain that brought memories of the resplendent temple In Jerusalem that was quickly becoming just a fading recollection in their tortured minds. What an awful price tag is attached to sin! What depths there are to which even the chosen of God can fall!

But why 70 years? Is there a special significance to that precise number of years for God's people to suffer under the Babylonian rule? To answer this question, we must remember a very important Bible principle. Nothing in the Word of God happens by chance. Everything has a very definite reason because God refuses to work in generalities, guesses, or approximations.

You will remember from your basic Bible study background that Israel enjoyed the promised land for 490 years, from the time of their exodus from Egypt until their exile in Babylon. God gave them a written law for the governing of the nation after their entrance into Canaan. This law was to be viewed in somewhat the same manner as a modem nation views its constitution. None of the precepts and guidelines could be ignored or violated without the backlash of appropriate penalties and punishments. One of these statements in the law of Israel concerned the use of the land and required that the land be given a sabbath of rest every 70 years:

"And the Lord spoke unto Moses in Mount Sinai, saying, speak unto the children of Israel, and say unto them, when ye come unto the land which I give you, then shall the land keep a sabbath unto the Lord. Six year: thou shalt sow thy field, and six years thou shalt prune thy vineyard, and gather in the fruit thereof but in the seventh year shall be a sabbath of rest unto the land, a sabbath for the Lord; thou shalt neither sow thy field, nor prune thy vineyard" (Leviticus 25:1-4).

The land was to rest! God commanded His people to let the land rest, but they refused to obey Him! Instead, they paid no regard at all to this apparently illogical directive of the Lord. After all, business is business, and it just made good business sense to continue working the land during the seventh year.

But how did God view that transgression? In Leviticus 26:32-35, God announces the awful penalty for violating the sabbath of the land:

"And I will bring the land into desolation: and your enemies who dwell therein shall be astonished at it. And I will scatter you among the heathen, and will draw out a sword after you; and your land shall be desolate, and your cities waste. THEN SHALL THE LAND ENJOY HER SABBATHS, as long as it lieth desolate, and ye are in your enemies land; even then shall the land rest, and enjoy her Sabbaths. As long as it did not rest in your sabbath, when ye dwell in it.""

In other words, God emphatically states in the above verses that He will not allow the land and His specific commands to be abused. This is a continuing principle that is true even in our own present age. It is true, for example, in reference to the stewardship of our money. God has reserved one-tenth of our income for Himself. If we obey Him and willingly return the tithe to Him, we will be abundantly blessed; if, however, we take the tithe for ourselves, God will resort to whatever means are necessary in order to retrieve it. You will not permanently retain that which belongs to God! Some Christians force the Lord to place them into conditions of sickness, financial adversity, or any number of other kinds of personal difficulties so that God's command about the tithe will be fulfilled. If you are saved, you will tithe, one way or the other!

How does this principle apply to the land? Israel had dwelled in Canaan, for 490 years. The requirement of God for them was that the land should rest every seventh year. Never once did His people obey this simple command. God's holiness demands that He must enforce every penalty that He has prescribed as punishment for every sin. Therefore, if you will take 490 years and divide it by seven years, the result is 70 years—the number of years the land would have rested if the Israelites had followed the plan of God. Hence, the children of Israel were forced off their homeland and placed into foreign exile until the 70 years were finished.

Daniel, Person of the Book

Unlike the unfounded opinions of weak Bible students who portray this book as one of gloom and doom, this historical and prophetic narrative from the hand of Daniel is actually one of the scriptures' most positive statements of human courage and faithfulness. The joy of sewing God is clearly outlined as the best of ways by which a man may live his life victoriously in spite of difficult surroundings. It is a very warm book, when read correctly, and God is seen in His full glory of tender compassion and divine justice. His overshadowing care and His love for faithful followers become the twin inheritances that He shares through the prophecies of His servant, Daniel.

What can be learned from this man, Daniel? The solid foundation and tough fiber of the Christ-life are best developed in the spiritual gymnasium of the soul where we are pushed to a point just beyond our individual limits and are placed in the critical position of suddenly realizing that unless God intervenes we have no hope. If you have been there, you know the sweet taste of triumph that is yours to savor as you emerge from the tunnel of tribulation with your hands held high, safe, and secure in the hand of God. If you have not been there, do not think of yourself as fortunate although in a human sense you are. You will never be as confident in the muscle of your faith until it is hardened in the arena of spiritual conflict where your heart repeatedly throbs a message "If God does not rescue me, I have no hope!" It was into just such a situation that Daniel finds himself because of the treachery of evil men.

Our childhood memories of favorite Bible characters and stories depict

Daniel as a young lad in his pre-teen years when he is confronted with the challenge of the den of lions. Millions of youthful believers have dared to be a Daniel after being thrilled by his unflinching resolve to do right. But historically, Daniel is a man steeped with advancing years, he is an old man, by the time that he is thrown to the lions. Remember, Daniel was taken captive in the invasion of Israel by Nebuchadnezzar in 607 B.C. Our best records of the time reveal that Darius came to rule in Babylon in the year 538 B.C., and it was during his reign that Daniel was ordered into the lions' den. Now, look to Daniel 1:3-4:

> "And the king spake to Ashpenaz the master of his eunuchs, that he should bring certain of the children of Israel, and of the kings seed, and of the princes, children in whom was no blemish, but well favored, and skillful in all wisdom, and cunning in knowledge, and understanding science, and such as had ability in them to stand in the king': palace, and whom they might teach the learning and the tongue of the Chaldeans. . . now among these were of the children of Judah, Daniel, Hananiah, Mishael, and Azariah. "

For young people to possess such obvious qualities and abilities, they must be at least in their middle teens to early twenties. Now, figure it out. Since Daniel was taken captive in 607 B.C. and the incident with the lions occurred in 5 38 B.C., we know that a span of 69 years was covered. If we allot Daniel a minimum age at his capture of 1 5 years and add that to the 69 years, it means that he had a minimum age of 84 years when he faced the lions. He was an old man! But he retained his youthful courage.

It is one of Christianity's greater principles that the power of God is readily available for any person of any age or state of physical health. No one is ever too young or too old to serve the Lord. Every saved person can be a victorious person. We can all be Daniels! It is entirely up to us!

Certain traits are found in the lives of Daniel and his three friends, Hananiah, Mishael, and Azariah. Daniel 1:4 says that they were:

> "Children in whom was no blemish, but well favored, and skillful, in all wisdom, and cunning in knowledge, and understanding science, and such as had ability in them to stand in the king': palace. and whom they might teach the learning and the tongue of the Chaldeans. "

As you look at this verse, five commendable attributes of these young men leap forth from the page. These faithful followers of God are presented as:

(1) SPOTLESS: *"...in whom was no blemish..."* What a grand statement affirming their outward testimony! To be without blemish in the Biblical sense is to have a holy lifestyle that cannot be attacked by the unbeliever or the skeptic. It is to be beyond reproach in the highest level of ethical and moral behavior. Such was the life of these men who had been careful to separate themselves from the evil influences of Satan and the flesh. Is not this also a mandate for the Christian? Paul says in I Corinthians 5:9-13:

"I wrote unto you in an epistle not to company with fornicators: yet not altogether with the fornicators of this world, or with the covetous, or extortionist, or with idolaters,-for then must ye needs go out of the world. But now ha ye I written unto you not to keep company, if any man that is called a brother be a fornicator, or covetous, or an idolater, or a railer, or a drunkard, or an extortioner, with such an one no not to ettt. For what hovel to do to judge them also that are without.' Do not ye judge them that are within? But them that are without God judgeth Therefore put away from among yourselves that wicked person."

And, in another place, Paul repeats this warning even more emphatically:

"Be ye not unequally yoked together with unbelievers: for what fellowship hath righteousness with unrighteousness? And what communion hath light with darkness7A nd what concord hath Christ with Belial? Or what part hath he that believeth with an infidel? For ye are the temple of the living God; As God hath said, I will dwell in them and walk in them; and I will be their God and they shall be my people. Where/"ore come out from among them, and be ye separate, saith the Lord; and touch not the unclean thing, and! will receive you. And will be a Father unto you, and ye shall be my sons and daughters, saith the Loni Almighty" (II Corinthians 6:14-18).

SPECIAL: *.. But well favored...* " (Daniel 1:4). Not only were these Godly men of Israel spotless, but they were also very special. They were approved. Even the pagan authorities in wicked Babylon were impressed with them. Our blessed Lord Jesus exhibited this same quality of appeal:

"And Jesus increased in wisdom and stature, and in favour with God and man" (Luke 2:52).

The Christ-life is best seen in the living of lives that are not so narrowly legalistic as to become thoroughly obnoxious; but on the contrary, our Lord is most often received by the unsaved when their witnesses are full of the graciousness and compassion of Christ.

(3) SKILLFUL: *. . skillful in all wisdom. . ."* (Daniel 1:4). Laziness was not at all a part of the personalities of these four young Israelites. They were all knowledgeable, as we shall see in a moment, but a person may be full of knowledge without possessing very much wisdom. In other words, he may have a full head and an empty heart. Wisdom is not common sense; it is uncommon sense. True wisdom cannot be acquired through Human effort but is divinely bestowed upon an individual by the Lord and is the vehicle by which a person has the necessary supernatural insights to make the right decisions that are necessary for a victorious life. Only God can grant that kind of wisdom.

"If any of you lack wisdom, let him ask of God. That giveth to all men liberally, and upbraideth not; and it shall be given him " (James 1:5).

(4) SMART: ". . . *and cunning in knowledge. . .* "(Daniel 1:4), There is absolutely no excuse for ignorance of God's Word. The major fundamental bedrock truths upon which the Christian faith is based can be quite well understood by mere children. We know that God is no respecter of persons. And that while there may be rather wide differences in learning abilities, He has nevertheless given a universal command for all of His children to study the Bible:

"Study to shew thyself approved unto God. a workman that needeth not Io be ashamed, rightly dividing the word of truth " (II Timothy 2:15).

(5) SELECTED: *. . and such as had ability in them to stand in the king's palace, and whom they might teach the learning and the tongue of the Chaldeans."* (Daniel 1:4). It has always amused and amazed me to watch God take extremely uncomfortable situations, such as the captivity of these Hebrew lads, and change everything for the good of the people involved. in fact, this sovereign control by

the Lord brings peace to the man who cannot see but still walks by faith alone into the darkness. God overrules the Evil One in those human affairs where the children of God are concerned. As I review my own personal journey with the Lord, it is apparent that the valleys of my life were training grounds for the later treks of exhilaration to the mountain peaks of victory for me and glory for Him!

As this first chapter of the Book of Daniel opens, we are introduced to these four Hebrew men about whom we have just been speaking. They are Daniel, Hananiah, Mishael, and Azariah. But verse seven tells us that their names were changed to Babylonian names by their captors:

Daniel became Belteshazzar;
Hananiah became Shadrach;
Mishael became Meshach;
Azariah became Abednego.

The Hebrew names were emblematic of their relationships To Jehovah God, and their Babylonian names must have been cruel insults to them in two significant ways. First, they were Stripped of their spiritual heritage because of the deep religious meanings of their Hebrew names. Second, they were forced to wear the names of pagan influence that represented everything that God s righteousness Opposed.

I think that it would be good at this point to examine these names in light of their original meanings. Daniel is "God will Judge"; his new name became Belteshazzar which was derived from 'the Babylonian god, Bel, and has an undetermined meaning. Hananiah is "the Lord is gracious"; his Babylonian name, Shadrach, also has an unknown meaning, Mishael, which means "'what the Lord is" became Meshach, another unknown meaning. Azariah tells that "the Lord helps" and his name became Abednego, or the "servant of Nego." Without question these name changes were nothing more than just another attempt to break the religious ties of these young men to the religion of their homeland.

"And the king appointed them a daily provision of the king's meat, and of the wine which he drank: so nourishing them three years. that at the end there of they might stand before the king. "

What a privilege! What a grand honor! Indeed, what a miracle! Here they are stranded in an alien country as virtual slaves, but suddenly they are brought by royal decree into an elevated position that affords them the luxury of dining upon the food of the king. So impressed was Nebuchadnezzar with them, he was intent upon supplying them with the necessary food to prepare them for standing "before the king," a reference to royal acceptance and prestige.

However, verse eight informs that *"Daniel purposed in his heart that he would not defile himself with the portion of the king': meat, nor with the wine which he drank. . . "* Perhaps this seems to border on fanaticism, but it really is not. The custom of the Babylonians was to worship their god, Bel, during their meals. Too, it was a general practice for them to dine upon the very meat that had been offered as a burned sacrifice to their false gods. To eat with the Babylonians would be to honor their paganism and these four Hebrew men were not about to compromise their faith in such evil practices. Paul makes clear that the consumption of sacrificial meat is strictly forbidden for the believer:

"What say I, then? That the idol is anything, or that which is offered in sacrifice to idols is anything? But I so y that the things which the Gentiles sacrifice, they sacrifice to devils, and not to God," and I would not that ye should have the fellowship with devils. Ye cannot drink the cup of the Lord, and the cup of the devils; ye cannot be partakers of the Lord': Table, and of the table of demons. Do we provoke the Lord to jealousy? Are we stronger than he? . . . But if any man say unto you, this is offered in sacrifice unto idols, eat not for his sake that showed it, and for conscience sake, for the earth is the Lord's, and the fullness thereof" (1 Corinthians 10: 1 9~22; 28-29).

Daniel and his friends were men who did not enjoy the light that belongs to our generation with its saturation of the gospel message via the mass media throughout the entire world. In fact, not only did they not even have a New Testament, but most of what we know as the Old Testament was also unknown to them. Yet, in spite of their lack of a complete Bible, these men knew the Lord. They were so intimately in tune with God that they daily practiced the words of I Corinthians 10:31:

"Whether therefore ye eat, or drink, or whatsoever ye do, do all to the glory of God. "

In Daniel 1:12-13 we come to a literary device known as an "anticipatory hint." As used here, this hint is a preview of Daniel's courage in accepting the challenges against him in later chapters. Daniel says to the prince of the eunuchs who is afraid to comply with the request of this consecrated Israelite:

"Prove thy servants, I beseech thee, ten days; and let them give us pulse to eat, and water to drink; then let our countenance; be looked upon before thee and the countenance of the children that eat of the portion of the king s meat; and as thou seest, deal with thy children. "

How similar these words are to the words of another prophet, Malaclu, who said: "Bring ye all the tithes into the storehouse, that there may be meat in mine house. and prove me now herewith. saith the Lord of hosts, if I will not open you the windows of heaven, and pour you out a blessing, that there shall not be room enough to receive it" (Malachi 3:10).

Our God has no fear whatever of the false gods of anyplace or any time. He is the Lord Omnipotent! He is the God All-Powerful! He delights in the flimsy and feeble challenges of these would-be deities! He relishes in the opportunity to manifest His power and glory over all the gods of this world. God is God! He encourages His children to put Him to the test!

Daniel's suggestion to the prince of the eunuch is well in line with God's taunt of His imposters like Bel, god of the Babylonians. Daniel proclaimed with total confidence in his Lord, "Prove thy servants. . . "Instead of the king's meat and wine, these four men of God want pulse (vegetables) and water. Then, after ten days a comparison examination could be made of them and of the other young men who ate from the king's table. The results were as expected:

"And at the end often days their countenances appeared fairer and fatter in flesh than all the children which did eat the portion of the king's meat" (Daniel 1:15).

A vital principle of the victorious lifestyle is the individual's willingness to refuse the comforts of this world in order to gain the approval of the next. Ours has been called a generation of convenience and the church of this age has been termed, "the cult of the comfortable." We would do well to recognize this lesson from Daniel and understand that prestige with this worldly system and power with God are not found in the Spirit-filled life.

Choices between the two are not always as easy as one might presume. Family pressure, peer group expectations, or personal ego (flesh) can be almost unbelievably persuasive to the believer who is trying to make decisions that will glorify God. Be a Daniel! Be true to God! He cannot, by His own holiness and truthfulness, ever let you down! Dear Reader, whatever tests the devil may place in your path will be to no avail if you will stand true to the convictions of your heart.

Faithfulness always brings its rewards. For Daniel and his friends, these blessings were at least six in number:

1) CONFERRAL OF GODLY GIFTS: *". . . God gave them knowledge and skill in all learning and wisdom: and Daniel had understanding in all visions and dreams" (1 : 1 7).*

Not only did God grant them knowledge in learning, but He also gave them skill in learning. How important! Especially in matters of the Christian faith, there can be found multitudes of sincere people who have a good grasp of the mechanics of the Scriptures but are unable to transfer that knowledge into a living reality and practice. Specifically, Daniel was given an understanding of visions and dreams. The Lord, because Daniel had passed the test at the king's table, set about to prepare this extraordinary young Israelite for the future task of speaking some of the Bible's greatest prophecies through his ability to interpret the visions and dreams of kings.

A rather insignificant incident, like Daniel's refusal to eat the king's food, can elevate the faithful follower to heights thought utterly unattainable. Jesus teaches this as a very important truth in Matthew 25:21 by declaring:

"His Lord said unto him, well done, thou good and faithful servant: thou has been faithful over a few things, I will make thee ruler over many things; enter thou into the joy of thy Lord. "

(2) COMMUNION WITH THE KING: "And the king communed with them . . ."(1:19). Please note that this is an illustration of the world seeking counsel from those who know God. Do you find this strange? You should not. Take an alcoholic who frequents the local taverns, for example. If he learns that he has only a short time to live, where does he go for consolation? Does he hurry to his drinking buddies? Oh no, he looks through tear-dimmed eyes for some sincere and committed Christian witness who can share with him how to have peace with God.

I do not find it strange that governmental leaders such as prime ministers, kings, and presidents often turn to men of God for advice and comfort. It is a wise public figure indeed who recognizes the need for God in the regulation of affairs over which he has ultimate responsibility. No accolade is as great as is the tribute of being looked upon as a man of God.

(3) CONVERSATION WITH THE KING: "*And in all matters of wisdom and understanding, that the king inquired of them . . .* "(1:20). These men were not only conferred gifts by the Lord and made participants in communion with the king, but they also had conversations with him. The word, "communed" (communion) speaks of very deep, serious and intense discussions; "inquired" speaks of more frequent dialogues. Truly consecrated followers of the Lord are so attractive that even their detractors enjoy being with them. The reasons are obvious. A well-balanced believer has a good blend of the humorous and pathos, the significant and insignificant, the complex and the simple in his conversations. Missing, however, are those verbal elements that are sordid, lewd, profane, ugly, negative, and
base. Even the world is impressed!

(4) COMPLIMENTS BY THE KING: "*. . . he found them ten times better than all the magicians and astrologers that were in all his realm* " (1:20). Let's face it! The difference between the advance of Western Civilization, principally in Europe and America, and the decline of other major world sectors such as the Far East and Middle East, can be almost totally laid to the factor of Christianity's influence in the West. Most major old-line universities and social benevolent societies were the offspring of Christian concern. The multitude of church spires that stand like a veritable forest of steeples across our country are a silent testimony to the national good that has been derived from the church. Secular sociologists are among the first to commend the social prosperity as having resulted from the influence of

Christianity; psychologists are aware and supportive of the need for a balanced spirit.

(5) CONTINUED IN THE LAND: *"And Daniel continued even unto the first year of King Cyrus"* (1:21). Remember, the length of the exile in Babylon was 70 years. It finally ended, as we shall see later in this study, with the invasion of the city by the combined forces of the Medes and Persians. Since Daniel lived to the reign of the Persian ruler, Cynis, it simply means that he survived this awful time of national judgment. He did not die in shame in the land of those who had overthrown his government and taken him captive.

With the conclusion of this first chapter of the book, we can see that Daniel and his friends are fully prepared for the eventualities that he ahead. They are equal to the tasks before them. Are you? Can you just as boldly face the uncertain days Through which you must pass? With Jesus, you can face tomorrow with confidence!

14 DANIEL

Chapter 2

The Dream of a King

Chapter two opens with our entrance into the sleeping quarters of the world's most powerful man of that particular day, King Nebuchadnezzar of the Babylonian Empire. So that you may be able to fully comprehend the magnitude of his authority, remember that the term, "empire," is the strongest and most all-inclusive descriptive word that can be used in reference to a nation. It is used correctly only when it is applied to a nation that has gained control of all its known world.

As we shall see later, Daniel accurately prophesied the number and identities of all of the empires that have ever existed up to this very day. These empires, in order of their appearances, have been the Babylonian, the Medo-Persian, the Grecian, and the Roman. One more empire is prophesied to come—the resurrected Roman Empire in league with ten nations under the diabolical leadership of the antichrist. Alter its demise, the universal rule of Jesus Christ in the Millennial Kingdom will abide for one thousand years.

But the Babylonian Empire, into which Daniel was taken captive, is the setting for this study. What was its origin? Who founded it? To answer these questions, we must turn back to Genesis 10:8-10:

"And Cush begat Nimrod; he began to be a mighty one in the earth. He was a mighty hunter before the Lord: wherefore it is said, Even as Nimrod the mighty hunter before the Lord. And the beginning of his kingdom was Babel . . ."

Do not think that this "mighty hunter" is a reference to the prowess of Nimrod in pursuit of wild animals; he was actually a bounty hunter of men according to a good definition of the word as it is used in the original language. This little city of Babel, the forerunner of the great Babylonian Empire, was founded by a ruthless killer.

To enter Babylon at the height of its glory must have been an unforgettable experience of beholding total opulence, massive architectural accomplishments, and splendor un-imaginable! Approaching the city, the traveler would first be amazed at the size of its outer wall. This wall measured 350 feet high and was 710 feet thick at the base but tapered to the top along which six teams of horses and chariots could run abreast. This wall surrounded the entire city which measured approximately 15 miles square. However, in the unlikely event that an invading army could penetrate or scale this outer wall, there was also an inner wall of some 250 feet in height from which the Babylonian defenders could pour boiling oil upon their attackers. What a virtually impenetrable city this was!

The primary entrance was through the Ishtar Gate which opened to the grand processional street that eventually led to the palace of Nebuchadnezzar. The gate, the street, and his palace walls were all decorated with huge sculptured lions.

Three complexes stand as monuments to the building skills of the Babylonians. First, and most famous, were the Hanging Gardens which have been designated as one of the eight wonders of the world. Nebuchadnezzar had taken to wife a woman of the Medes who became homesick for the mountains of her native land. Obviously, he could not establish his permanent residence in the land of Medea, so he determined to bring the mountains to Babylon. He developed the Hanging Gardens, a multi-tiered structure that was filled with an almost endless variety of flowers, fruit trees, and assorted exotic plants. One of the intriguing questions for students of the period pertains to the method of cultivation that resulted in the growth of plants that were imported to the area from alien climates. Walking through the gardens must have been a breath-taking experience indeed.

The second building of note was the Temple Tower which was actually a step-pyramid, or ziggurat. A ziggurat is constructed with a large foundation at the base with a slightly smaller level laid on top of that base and a slightly smaller level than the second level laid next. The ancient historian, Herodotus, says that Nebuchadnezzar's Temple Tower rose to a step- pyramid (ziggurat) height of eight such levels.

Marduk's Temple was the third of the identifiable buildings that has been uncovered in Babylon. To a great extent, it was designed similar to some of our more modem downtown skyscrapers, with compartmentalized rooms through-out. Some have suggested that this temple was probably the site of Belshazzar's feast that we will see later in this study.

It was a huge building, measuring over one mile long and 1600 feet wide. Around the outside of this massive structure were 5400 pillars styled in the shape of plaster elephants covered in gold-leaf. Astride each elephant sat a bronze gladiator. The citizens of this ancient city must have swelled with nationalistic pride as they viewed this long row of gladiator columns. Certainly, in their minds, there was no reason to fear the sword of any other nation on the face of the earth as long as they were surrounded by such obvious evidences of their wealth and military superiority.

With the setting for the opening chapters well-fixed in your mind, let us now move to the bedside of a restless and troubled King Nebuchadnezzar in chapter two. The most powerful man on earth with limitless wealth experienced the same fears of the future as a pauper in his shack. It is a timeless lesson of universal application that every person who treads upon the soil of this earth will at some point in his life be confronted by two disconcerting questions. Where is this world headed? What is going to happen to me? No man, not even a king, is exempted from pondering these same thoughts. In anxious contemplation, he called upon his trusted advisers to interpret his dreams:

"Then the king commanded to call the magicians, and the astrologers, and the sorcerers, and the Chaldeans, for to shew the king his dreams. So they came and stood before the king" (2:2).

This pagan king needed help, and he turned to men of this world's dark and seamy side for relief. Even in our enlightened age, immature believers will trudge off to séances, palm readers, and fortune-tellers. With unbridled excitement and a little bit of resentment toward my skepticism they exclaim, "But, Dr. Hunter, these people told me things about my life that they could not possibly have known, there must be something to it!"

There is something to it, all right! It will be a glad day in the church of the Lord Jesus Christ when we learn that everything that is spiritual is not necessarily Godly. Just as there is a Holy Spirit of God, there is also an unholy spirit of the devil whose intention it is to confuse and frustrate the believer. What does the Bible say about the kinds of counselors that Nebuchadnezzar called upon for advice?

"When thou art come in the land which the Lord thy God giveth thee, thou shalt not learn to do after the abominations of those nations. There shall not be found among you any one that maketh his son or daughter to pass through the fire, or that useth divination, or an observer of times, or an enchanter, or a witch, or a necromancer. For all that do these things are an abomination unto the Lord; and because of these abominations the Lord thy God doth drive them out from before thee" (Deuteronomy 18:9-12).

One group of the king's advisers were the astrologers. Astrology and astronomy are not at all the same. Astronomy is the legitimate scientific study of the actual physical stars in the universe, but astrology is the assigning of abstract meanings and prophecies to the various positions and alignments of the stars. "Astra" means "star"; "logos" means "word." Astrology is, therefore, "the word of the stars." As a believer, which do you prefer, the Word of God or the word of the stars? Read Isaiah's rebuke:

"Thou are wearied in the multitude of thy counsels. Let now the astrologers, the stargazers, the monthly prognosticators, stand up, and save thee from those things that shall come upon thee. Behold, they shall be as stubble; the fire shall burn them; they shall not deliver themselves from the power of the flame: there shall not be a coal to warm at, nor fire to sit before it" (Isaiah 47:13-14)

As you continue reading chapter two of Daniel, the story takes an unusual turn. It seems that the king forgot his dream but evidently remembered that it was a horrifying nightmare. The Chaldeans optimistically proclaim in verse four: . ."Tell thy servants the dream, and we will shew the interpretation. " Anybody, even a mental dunce, could give some kind of interpretation.

But a problem arises! As mentioned already, the king could not recall the nature of his dream, so he threatened those pretenders of wisdom:

". . . the thing is gone from me: if ye will not make known unto me the dream, with the interpretation thereof, ye shall be cut in pieces, and your houses shall be a dunghill. But if ye shew the dream, and the interpretation thereof, ' ye shall receive of me gifts and rewards and great honor: therefore shew me the dream, and the interpretation thereof" (2:5-6).

Of course, the magicians and astrologers immediately recognized their plight. They were between the proverbial "rock and a hard place." Their only defense was to excuse themselves by asserting that there was not a person on the earth who could fulfill the request of the king. Such feeble attempts to cover-up their ridiculous fakery infuriated Nebuchadnezzar:

"For this cause the king was angry and furious, and commanded to destroy all the wise men of Babylon. And the decree went forth that the wise men should be slain; and they sought Daniel and his fellows to be slain " (2:12-13).

Are Daniel, Shadrach, Meshach, and Abenego in deep trouble? From the viewpoint of the world, these men were the unfortunate victims of cruel circumstances. For the followers of our Sovereign Lord of Glory, however, there are no accidents or unforeseen coincidences. Everything in the believer's life is according to divine plan and the providential hand of God:

"For we know that all things work together for good to them that love God, to them who are the called according to his purpose. " (Romans 8:28).

God was busy putting Daniel in a place of Babylonian exaltation. Someone has said that God takes the axe that the devil has sharpened to cut off Satan's head. In verses 14-18, Daniel met the problem with confidence rather than fleeing from it. In so doing, he left all of us who love God and yet find ourselves in dire predicaments a pattern by which we can overcome the snares of the devil. After he had consulted with Arioch, the captain of the guard, whose responsibility it had become to execute Daniel, this faithful man of God:

> *DEFINED HIS PROBLEM:* "Then Daniel went in, and desired of the king that he would give him time, and that he would shew the king the interpretation" (verse 16). Daniel walked straight into the most dangerous of all places for him—the throne room of the king. He did not waver and he did not faint. Daniel learned first-hand all that he could about the challenge before him. He did not let his fears control his thoughts; he let his thoughts control his fears. Sometimes we have irrational thoughts of sheer terror because we have not first defined our problems.

DISCUSSED HIS PROBLEM: "*Then Daniel went to his house, and made the thing known to Hananiah, Mishael, and Azariah, his companions" (verse 17)*. It always helps to share the pains and problems that we are bearing with those trusted friends who have shown themselves to be compassionate and understanding on previous occasions. Their empathy and insight and prayer support can be beyond value during days of darkness.

DESIRED AN ANSWER: "*That they would desire mercies of the God of heaven concerning this secret; that Daniel and his fellows should not perish with the rest of the wise men of Babylon " (verse 18)*. Together these men turned to God in prayer. They had faithfully adhered to a golden principle: "Work like everything depends on you. But pray like everything depends on God. "All that was possible for Daniel to do he had done. Now, it was up to the Lord!

After Daniel and his friends had met God in earnest prayer, verse 19 informs us that "then was the secret revealed unto Daniel in a night vision. "Upon receiving from the Lord the miraculous answer to his pleadings, what did Daniel do? Did he first shout praises to God? No, he did not! Did he awaken his sleeping friends and gladly share the good news? No, he did not! Did he run to Arioch, the captain of the king's guard, and demand an immediate audience with Nebuchadnezzar? No, he did not! Instead, Daniel "*blessed the God of heaven*" (verse 19).

One of the marks of a Godly man is his deep gratitude for whatever is given him by the Lord or by his friends. Before Daniel sprang into action with the correct interpretation of the king's dream, he stated two important elements of the principle of appropriation during his brief season of thanksgiving.

First, he accepted as an absolute and undeniable fact that ". . . *wisdom and might. . .* "belong to God (verse 20). For the believer, the wisdom of God means "*the ability to fully understand anything*" and the might of God means "*the ability to do everything.*" This first point in the principle of appropriation is the theological position.

Second, we are told in verse 23 that Daniel thanks God because He ". . .

hast given me wisdom and might, and hast made known unto me now what we desired of thee: for thou hast now made known unto us the king's matter: "This second point in the principle of appropriation is the practical position. Biblical truths are not for mental assent alone; they are to be "lived out" in the believer's life.

Now that we know that Daniel was granted the wisdom and might of God, it helps us understand why verse 24 begins with the word, "therefore":

"*THEREFORE Daniel went unto Arioch, whom the king had ordained to destroy the wise men of Babylon: he went and said thus unto him, destroy not the wise men of Babylon: bring me in before the king, and I will shew unto the king the interpretation.*"

Boldness in the face of fierce opposition comes rather easily to the man who is dressed in the garments of God's wisdom and might. Neither the king nor his captain posed a problem for Daniel. The sovereign care of the Almighty encircled him. Dear Reader, never despair when threatened by the hounds of hell. Be like Daniel who did not flee in fear nor tried to fight in his human strength. Learn to call upon God and wait for His definite directions. Following Him, no enemy can prevail!

A comparison of the temporary and the eternal was given by Daniel in verses 27-28. Standing before the king, he reminded Nebuchadnezzar of the failure of the wise men of Babylon to determine and interpret the dream. Triumphantly, Daniel proclaims in verse 28, "*But there is a God in heaven. . .* "Oh, how grand is this promise! Whatever our personal plight, there is a place toward which we may turn for consolation and support. Yes, there is a God in heaven!

You will note the phrase, ". . . in the latter days . . ." found in verse 28. This is a recurring phrase in the Old Testament that always is used in reference to prophecies of the end-time. The use of that phrase here in chapter two of the Book of Daniel confirms that the king's dream was actually a prophecy that is yet to be completely fulfilled.

To summarize this famous dream, the king, as he slept, had seen the image of a man with a gold head, arms of silver, torso of brass, legs of iron, and feet of iron and clay. Suddenly, he saw a little stone cut out of a mountain come hurtling through the air to smash the feet of the image. The stone then grew into a mountain itself and filled the whole earth.

Again, the passage is provided with a clear interpretation in later verses:

FIRST WORLD EMPIRE IS BABYLONIAN: *"Thou, O king art a king of kings . . . thou art this head of gold..."* *(Daniel 2:37, 39).*

SECOND WORLD EMPIRE IS MEDO-PERSIAN: *".. And after thee shall arise another kingdom inferior to thee. . . "(Daniel 2:39).* History records that a combined army of the Medes and the Persians diverted the water of the Euphrates River from flowing under the wall of the city of Babylon, thereby cutting off its water supply and leaving a passage way under the wall to invade the city. They entered and defeated the Babylonians.

THIRD WORLD EMPIRE IS GRECIAN: *". . . and another kingdom of brass which shall bear rule over all the earth "(Daniel 2:39).* Alexander the Great led the Greeks on a rampage through the world, destroying every nation that resisted him. One of his finest hours was when he could finally exclaim at the age of thirty-three, "How sad that there are no more worlds to conquer!"

FOURTH WORLD EMPIRE IS ROMAN: *". . . and the fourth kingdom shall be as strong as iron . .* (Daniel 2:40). The legs of iron picture the Roman Empire. Someone might question that interpretation since there were two legs; but remember that the Roman Empire was divided into two grand divisions with the western sector of the empire and its capital of Rome and the eastern sector of the empire and its capital of Constantinople. The ten toes are an extension of the influence of the old Roman Empire. Each toe represents a nation in the ten-country confederation of nations that will be under the leadership of the antichrist from his headquarters in Rome. In verse 42, you will note that 'the toes are part of iron and part of clay, indicating that just as the old Roman Empire was outwardly strong in its military (iron), it was inwardly weak in its lack of character and discipline (clay). Eventually, at the end of time, the last great world ruler called "the antichrist," will see his kingdom crumble from within. See Revelation 17.

(5) FINAL WORLD EMPIRE: THE MILLENIAL KINGDOM: "*And in the days of these kings shall the God of heaven set up a kingdom, which shall never be destroyed: and the kingdom shall not be left to other people, but it shall break in pieces and consume all these kingdoms, and it shall stand forever*" *(Daniel 2:44).* This verse is in reference to the little stone cut from the mountain mentioned earlier. As it fills the whole earth, it replaces all other nations and empires with its power. Verse 44 is quite clear that this will be the final empire for it shall "*never be destroyed: and the kingdom shall not be left to other people . . .*"

In verse 45, the stone is a reference to the virgin-born Jesus Christ for it is said that the stone. . "*was cut out of the mountain without hands . .* The coming of Jesus into the world was not at all the doing of man; the birth of our Lord remains totally unexplainable by the measure of the human mind. He is our Rock of Ages; He is our Cornerstone!

In verse 45, there are two words of significance: "*and the dream is CERTAIN: and the interpretation thereof is SURE.* " We must always enter spiritual battle with the sublime confidence that the Word of God shall not fail. Daniel was armed in a way that the Chaldeans, astrologers, and sorcerers were not. Theirs was a cunning skill developed from the wisdom of this world; his was a reliance upon the trustworthiness of our Lord. Within himself lay no abilities greater than that of any other member of the human family. He well understood that man's extremity is the point of God's beginning. When backed into a comer with nowhere else to turn for escape, man has only to find sweet refuge in Jesus and a supply of strength for the meeting of any adverse situations will be readily granted him. As long as an individual believes that there might just be something else that he can do to remedy his own desperate straits, God will let him. It is equally true for the unsaved man that God will not save him until that man recognizes the futility of all other methods of salvation. As the hymn writer has said:

My hope is built on nothing less Than Jesus' blood and righteousness; I scarce not trust the sweetest frame. But wholly lean on Jesus' name.

A condition of instability and wavering exists in the modern church. Is it not an unsettling reality that this has resulted from too much organizing in the basement and not enough agonizing in the upper room? Are we not as incapable and inept against the prince of darkness as a battalion of wooden soldiers? So much that we do, presumably in the name of Jesus, is in actuality done in the energy of the flesh, performed to the exact concepts and designs of human imaginations. Such religious game-playing deadens the church and paralyzes the only organization in the world that has the capacity to be more than just another organization in the world. Operating by the dictates of human ingenuity, the church proceeds into its endeavors with caution and a sense of tentativeness because it is following "majority reports" or the "best estimates." Be it well understood! The church is not a democracy, it is a dictatorship with Christ as its head! Nothing should ever be attempted without the absolute certainty of His consent.

"Hast thou faith? Have it to thyself before God. Happy is he that condemneth not himself in that thing which he alloweth. And he that doubteth is damned if he eat, because he eateth not of faith; for whatsoever is not of faith is sin "(Romans 14:22-23).

As Daniel, we should always labor in the climate of God's one hundred percent approval and endorsement. If there are doubts at all, we should recognize those questions as spiritual signals of potential danger. Frequently, as a pastor, I am asked if cigarette smoking or high school dancing or some other social activity may be sinful. My first response is always, "If you must ask whether it is right or wrong then it must be wrong, because whatever we do should be done in absolute faith, or else it is wrong."

In verses 46-49 of the second chapter of Daniel, we see the rare picture of the world's most royal and powerful leader on his face before a lowly slave. Note in verse 46 that Nebuchadnezzar ". . . *worshipped Daniel* . . ."Too often the messenger becomes the object of adoration instead of the One who sent the message. No worse insult is suffered by the sincere preacher than for those among whom he ministers to elevate him above their own love for God. With the departure of the faithful preacher from a pastorate, there will also be a departure of many of his flock from the fold of that church. Often this exodus develops because of an enthusiasm for their previous pastor's style or personality. Such displaced devotion ought not to be!

In verse 47, Nebuchadnezzar described God with three statements that displayed his own awareness of the character of the God of the Israelites in contrast to the gods of the Babylonians. He recognized that God is:

(l) GLORIOUS: *. . your God is a God of gods. .* (verse 47). Nebuchadnezzar's background was that of poly- theism;"poly" means "many" and "the" means "god." His was a religion that included respect for many gods. With this presentation by Daniel, the king admitted the superiority of Jehovah over the other gods of the nations. "God of gods" conveys the belief that the highest powers of heaven must pay homage to God. In Nebuchadnezzar's religious system of mythological gods, there was a hierarchy of positions of power among the various deities. His description of Jehovah as "God of gods" means that he was now convinced that all the gods must bow before the glorious God of Daniel.

> GREAT: *. . and a Lord of kings. . .*" (verse 47). Most ancient monarchs looked upon themselves as gods. Even °'"_°Even their opponents within their kingdoms were hesitant to decry the likelihood of divine power upon the throne. It was a confession of considerable magnitude, therefore, when Nebuchadnezzar alluded to God as "Lord of kings." Even as he believed that the gods of heaven were subservient to Jehovah, even so he believed that the "gods" of earth were also in subjection to the Lord.

(3) GRACIOUS: "*. . . and a revealer of secrets, seeing thou couldest reveal this secret "(verse 47)*. Nebuchadnezzar's was a world in which the gods were not fountains of grace but were, instead, reservoirs of greed. Men served in fear with little good returned to them, with the possible exception of a semblance of peace with their gods by some method of placating them, such as the use of human sacrifice. What an unbelievable revelation to Nebuchadnezzar that the God of Daniel would so graciously speak with him and care for him.

Please note in verse 47 that the king referred to Jehovah as "your God." In spite of his recognition of God as God, Nebuchadnezzar was still unable to personally embrace Him. It is a frequent and sad reaction by lost men to the wooing of the Spirit of our Lord. Without hesitation, many will acknowledge Him as Lord with their lips but not with their hearts. Having been so impressed with Daniel, Nebuchadnezzar expressed his admiration for this humble man of God in three ways. He made Daniel:

(1) RESPECTED: "*Then the king made Daniel a great man . . .* "(verse 48). The Babylonians who had earlier scorned him now revered him. Those who had been under command to execute him, now exalted him. Everywhere he went, there must have been excited whispers of wonder at such an unbelievable promotion. No longer was Daniel counted among the slaves; he was now numbered with the sovereign. He would now be seen associating with different people, discussing different matters, and wearing different garments. All of this resulted from a gracious gift of God to him. Is this not also time for the slave to sin who becomes a child of the King because of God's grace? He has a new position, - a new conversation, and a new appearance:

"Therefore, if any man be in Christ, he is a new creature. Old things are passed away; behold, all things are become new" (II Corinthians 5:17).

RICH: *. . and gave him many great gifts . .*" (verse 48). Here was a pauper made wealthy. Not only as he respected, but he was also rich. Perhaps, Dear Reader, you have few material possessions in this world, but it would do you well to remember that our Risen Christ has made you rich:

"But unto every one of us is given grace according to the measure of the gilt of Christ. Wherefore, he saith, when he ascended up on high, he led captivity captive, and gave gifts unto men" (Ephesians 4:7-8).

Be well assured that the temporal riches of this age cannot compare with the grace-gifts of the Father so abundantly given His children. You are rich! You are the child of the King!

(3) RULER: *. . and made him ruler over the whole province of Babylon, and chief of the governors over all the wise men of Babylon "* (verse 48). That which had ruled over Daniel was now ruled by him. A personal application of that same Biblical precept applies to the believer.

"For sin shall not have dominion over you; for ye are not under the law but under grace" (Romans 6:14).

Finally, in verse 49, Daniel again displays more traits of the man of God. Although he had been elevated to a status of prestige, he did not forget his friends who had so willingly and faithfully labored with him in prayer. All too often, even in the world of religion, prominence becomes the breeding ground of personal pride and a sense of disdain for past roots. How refreshing it is to have sweet fellowship with an individual who has been the grateful recipient of large divine blessings and still retains the humility of his origins! Someone has well-said that you can never know how poor you are until you meet someone to whom worldly riches mean absolutely nothing.

Not only did Nebuchadnezzar place Shadrach, Meshach, and Abendego over the "*affairs of the province of Babylon*" (verse 49), but he also allowed Daniel to sit "in the gate of the king" (verse 49). The gate was the Old Testament place of honor, decision making and municipal authority. Backslidden Lot sat in the gate of Sodom and Gomorrah and lost commitment to the God of his father, Abraham. Not so with Daniel! As we shall see later, he never once compromised his convictions.

28 DANIEL

Chapter Three

The Fiery Furnace

As the second chapter closed, we saw a king come close to the point of making Daniel's God his God. If no more had been said of Nebuchadnezzar than what we read in those verses, we would have left him with the conviction that he surely must have become a believer very soon thereafter. Unfortunately, chapter three opens with him departing" from his previous declaration of Jehovah as "Gods of gods and Lord of kings." He had turned to idolatry and the erection of a god of gold.

In so doing, Nebuchadnezzar pictures the image of the final world-ruler, the antichrist (the beast) of Revelation. Daniel 3:1 says:

"Nebuchadnezzar the king made an image of gold, whose height was threescore cubits, and the breadth thereof six cubits; he set it up in the plain of Dara, in the province of Babylon. "

Note the size of the image. It was threescore cubits tall; it was six cubits wide, the numbers are eerily significant (60+6; 66). How similar to the mark of the beast in Revelation 13, which is the number 666. Lest you think the comparison between the two images is reading too much into the Scriptures, note the words of Revelation 13:11-15:

"And I beheld another beast coming up out of the earth; and he had two horns like a lamb, and he spoke as a dragon. And he exerciseth all the power of the first beast before him, and causeth the earth and them which dwell therein to worship the first beast whose deadly wound was healed. A nd he doeth great wonders, so that he makethjire come down from heaven on the earth in the sight of men. And deceiveth them that dwell on the earth by the means of those miracles which he had power to do in the sight of the beast; saying to them that dwell on the earth, that they should make an image to the beast, which had the wound by a sword, and did live. And he had power to give life unto the image to the beast, which had the wound by a sword, and did live. And he had power to give life unto the image of the beast, that the image of the beast should both speak, and cause that as many as would not worship the image of the beast should be killed. "

Moreover, it must also be remembered that the name of the political and economic system of the antichrist, where this false image in Revelation will be constructed will be called by the name of Babylon.

Returning to the third chapter of Daniel, we notice an almost identical statement being made four times. That statement first appears in verse five:

"That at what time ye hear the sound of the comet, flute. harp, sackbut, psaltery, dulcimer, and all kinds of musical, ye fall down and worship the golden image that Nebuchadnezzar the king hath set up. "

That proclamation by the king's herald is repeated in verses 7, 10, and 15. Why is this of importance?

Music in worship is predominately an Old Testament activity. In our day, praise fests and celebration services are replacing the emphasis upon the preaching of the Word. Almost all, I could say all, the leaders of such services find their scriptural support in the Old Testament more than in the New Testament. Although I enjoy musical presentations and derive great benefit from them, I must remind you that there is an emphasis upon music in the modern church that cannot find foundation in the New Testament.

If we would be honest, there is no activity in the church that is more vulnerable to the subtle use of Satan than is the music program because of its very nature. Small and large churches alike find themselves embroiled in bitter conflicts over personality clashes among those who are participants in music groups. This should not surprise us, however, because Satan was in charge of ' the music in heaven before his banishment to this world. Note Ezekiel 28:13:

"Thou has been in Eden. the garden of God." every precious stone was thy covering, the sardius, topaz, and the diamond, the beryl, the onyx, and the jasper, the sapphire, the emerald, and i the carbunele, and gold; the workmanship of thy tabrets arid of pipes WAS PREPARED IN THEE IN THE DAY THAT THOU WAST CREATED. "

Another similarity between Nebuchadnezzar and the antichrist of the end-time is that both are world leaders who force religion upon the general populace. Daniel 3:5-6 says of Nebuchadnezzar's decree:

" . . . ye fall down and worship the golden image that Nebuchadnezzar, the king, hath set up. And whosoever falleth, not down and worshipeth, shall the same hour be cast into the midst of a burning fiery furnace. "

And what of the antichrist and his state religion? Revelation 13:7-8 informs us:

"And it was given unto him to make war with the saints, and to overcome them; and power was given him over all kindreds, and tongues, and nations. And all that dwell upon the earth shall worship him, whose names are not written in the book of Life of the Lamb slain from the foundation of the world."

Do you remember the Chaldeans who had been exposed as fakers and charlatans before the king by Daniel? Still stinging from barbs of the kings rebuke,, they had been lying in wait for a chance to get revenge. Verse eight shares:

"Wherefore. at that time. certain Chaldeans came near and accused the Jews. "

Problems. serious problems. will come to all of God's children. We cannot pretend that dark days do not arrive in the lives of God's choicest saints. Just because we have life in Christ, we are not exempted from the sorrows as those who know not the Lord. It would be good for us, therefore, to learn how we ought to view the pains we are called upon to endure. Our sufferings will arrive from one of two sources primarily.

(1) TEMPTATIONS OF SATAN: Much of the hurt we have felt came either directly or indirectly from the devil, but in a very real sense, we "brought it on ourselves." Listen to James as he warns us:

"Let no man say when he is tempted, I am tempted of Gad; for God cannot be tempted with evil, neither tempteth he any man; but every man is tempted, when he is drawn away of his own lust, and enticed" (James 1:13-14).

In other words, Satan can no more make a person do that which is evil than Jesus can cause a man to do that which is right. By the exercise of his own will, a man either yields to, or overcomes, the temptations of Satan. If he yields, trouble becomes his immediate and painful reward.

(2) TESTINGS OF THE SAVIOR: Sometimes God leads us in a path of His choosing that will bring us face-to-face with situations that may seem insurmountable by our own estimations. A good example was the incident at the Red Sea for the children of Israel as they were leaving Egypt. God had known all along that the route He was guiding them would apparently dead-end at the sea. He was trying to place them into a position of total dependency upon Him for relief so that they would find that He never fails.

The pressure was on the three Hebrew lads. They were commanded to bow before the image or suffer a torturous death in the fiery furnace. More than a temptation of the devil, this comes as a testing of God. Sadly, most of those affiliated with the modem church would fail the test. Some would reason that it would be better in the long-term for them to remain alive. That nothing could be accomplished by their deaths. Others would justify their bowing to the image by explaining that down deep inside they did not really mean it. For these Hebrew lads, it was
a clear black and white decision. Please note their reply to the king in verse 16:

"Shadraeh. Meshach, and Abednego answered and said to the king, O Nebuchadnezzar, WE ARE NOT CAREFUL TO ANSWER THEE IN THIS MATTER."

Like Daniel before Nebuchadnezzar, these fearless followers of the Lord were not hesitant at all to boldly proclaim their unshakeable commitment to follow God, whatever the cost. We are seeing in recent days an alarming preponderance Of electronic evangelists who promise a life of no-pain and all- case for the saints who exhibit sufficient faith. They would have us believe that no serious difficulties will ever engulf the man whose faith is fixed on the Lord. Oh, how thankful I am for like that of Shadrach, Meshach, and Abednego:

"If it be so, our God, whom we serve, is able to deliver us from the burning fiery furnace, and he will deliver us out of thine hand, O king. But if not, be it known unto thee, O king, that we will not serve thy gods, nor worship the

golden image which thou hast set up"(Daniel 3:1 7-18).

No stipulations, no bargains, were made by these men upon the plan of God for their lives. Whatever He wanted, they wanted. The singular mark of the truly spiritual man is his complete submission, his spirit of utter yieldedness to the will of God. We must pass that joyful allegiance to divine will from our heart to the hearts of the next generation as a priceless heritage.

From the Old South of the United States comes an old fable of Brer Rabbit and the briar patch from the series of stories about Uncle Remus. It seems that Brer Rabbit was finally captured through the trickery of his arch-enemy, Brer Fox. As Brer Fox was carrying his prisoner away, he begins to think about the various ways he can cause his old nemesis to suffer. When he mentions the river, Brer Rabbit happily agrees that he deserves to be thrown into the river, but he begs to be spared the fate of the briar patch. Other methods of painful death are discussed, Brer Rabbit gladly agrees with all of them but pleads for mercy instead of being cast into the briar patch. Finally, Brer Fox smiles a sly grin and with a great heave he hurls Brer Rabbit into the briar patch, who upon landing, goes singing on his way.

The very best place for Shadrach, Meshach, and Abednego was the fiery furnace. Why? Very simply, that was the place where God had an appointment to meet them. To remain physically comfortable outside the furnace would have caused them to miss one of the grandest, and rarest, of Old Testament occurrences, a visit with the pre-incarnate Lord Jesus Christ. Sometimes we so frantically plead for a life devoid of problems, and yet it may be in the dark pit of life's harrowing experiences that we truly meet God.

Here are only a few of God's best followers who found that it was better to face problems with the Lord than to face tranquility without Him:
1) Abel met a violent death;
2) Noah suffered ridicule as he built an ark for the most fearsome flood of all time;
(3) Abraham lifted the dagger to kill his only son;
(4) The mother of Moses tearfully placed him in a woven basket among the bulrushes;
(5) Moses suffered the deprivation of Egypt's wealth and glory as he turned to the wilderness;

6) Joshua risked rejection as he led his people around the walls of Jericho;
(7) Shamgar had only an ox-goad with which to defend himself against 600 Philistines;
(8) David fought the giant with a slingshot;
(9) Hezekiah was surrounded by 185,000 soldiers in Sennacherib's army.

Bound in the clothes they wore, these faithful Hebrews were cast into a furnace that was heated seven times hotter than was ordinary. In fact, the furnace was so hot that the men who had been chosen to cast the king's captives into the fire were themselves slain by the heat (verse 22).

Now, a miracle occurred before the very eyes of Nebuchadnezzar. He jumped to his feet and exclaimed, ". . . *Did not we three men bound, into the midst of the fire? They and said unto the king, true, oh king*"(verse 24). Nebuchadnezzar was astounded at what was transpiring before his very eyes.

"He answered and said, Lo, I see four men loose, walking in the midst of the fire. and they have no hurt; and the form of the fourth is like the Son of God "(verse 25).

Three things of significance were said of the Hebrew men in this verse:

(1) THEY WERE LOOSE: There was greater liberty inside the furnace than outside, as previously discussed. This is also true of the Christian faith itself. The agnostic sees only the bondage of "thou-shalt-not." He wants nothing to do with such a restrictive lifestyle. He cannot understand that the things he views as restrictions are actually disciplines that provide freedom. Because an accomplished pianist has learned the disciplines of the piano, he has liberty in making the instrument respond to his every touch. The person who is not guided by piano disciplines can never play it. So, which of the two is free?

THEY WERE WALKING: Running denotes momentary enthusiasm. Standing still conveys the idea of resignation. Walking suggests deliberate, long-lasting action. Have you ever noticed Isaiah 40:31?

"But they that wait upon the Lord shall renew their strength; they shall mount up with wings as eagles; they shall run. And not be weary: they shall walk. and not

faint. "

Very few times do we have experiences of exhilaration in our lives in which we soar with joyful glee. Weddings, birth, and special honors bring that kind of elation that we describe as being "on cloud nine."

Very few times do we have experiences of short duration in which we are called upon to expend more than our ordinary energy to complete an endeavor. Formal education exercises, pursuit of a particular job opportunity, and the solving of problems are examples of times that we do more than is required for a desired conclusion.

Many times, in fact virtually all of our lives, will be spent in walking through the circumstances of our day-to-day routines. We plod along, not on eagle's wings nor runner's feet. Far more Christian character and personal commitment must be present for the multitude of small decisions that we face every waking hour of every day than is necessary for the infrequent times of rising enthusiasm or exhaustive dashes.

The Hebrew lads were walking, apparently in contemplative meditation upon the Lord. They were secure, they were safe, in the protective custody of a God who is always touched with the feeling of His children's infirmities and cares.

(3) THEY WERE UNHURT: With the king as a spectator of what had been anticipated as a torturous death, these three faithful men were unharmed at all. So complete was their physical deliverance that verse 27 shares with us these words.

"And the princes, governors, and captains, and the king': counselors, being gathered together, saw these men. Upon whose bodies the fire had no power, nor was an hair of their head singed, neither were their coats changed. nor the smell of
fire had passed on them. "

This verse should be read as a beautiful illustration of justification which occurs simultaneously with salvation. There is a difference between these two blessed doctrines. Let me use another example to clarify these grand truths. If I pull a man from a deep and muddy pond, I have saved him. That is salvation. Jesus pulled us from certain destruction in hell. If I take the man that I pulled from the pond to my home, allow him to bathe, and launder his clothes, he will have the appearance of a person that has not been in the pond at all. That is justification. God not only saves us from the penalty of sin, but he also presents us without any taint of stain of sin. It is indeed "just-as-if-I'd" never sinned. When Shadrach, Meshach, and Abednego emerged from the furnace, no one could have possibly known by any evidence whatever that they had just been inside a place of fire-not so much as a single eyebrow. Bless God, when we are saved and justified, the marks of previous sins are thoroughly washed away by the blood of our Lord. Many passages might be cited in support of this wondrous truth, but one will suffice.

"I have blotted out, like a thick cloud, thy transgressions, and like a cloud. thy sins. . (Isaiah 44:22)

As earlier in chapter two in his experience with Daniel, Nebuchadnezzar was over-awed by the realization that God had intervened for Shadrach, Meshach, and Abednego:

"Then Nebuchadnezzar spoke, and said. blessed be the God of Shadrach. Meshach, and Abednego, who hath sent his angel, and delivered his servants that trusted in him, and have changed the king's word, and yielded their bodies, that they might not serve nor worship any god, except their own God. " (3:28)

What a tremendous confession of the protective care of our Lord! For the second time in this Book of Daniel ,Nebuchadnezzar has been brought to a concrete awareness of the reality and all- sufficiency of God. More than all of the other vile sins in his life stands this rejection of God as his greatest act of wickedness. Please understand that to sin against light is the most abominable of all man's transgressions. Greater than murder, or rape, or child-abuse, or sexual perversion is this frequently committed sin. Does this seem strange and unreasonable? Listen to the words of our Savior as He speaks to the decent and socially cultured people of Capernaum in Matthew 11:23-24:

"And thou, Capernaum, which are exalted unto heaven, shalt be brought down to hell; for if the mighty works, which have been done in thee, had been done in Sodom, it would have remained until this day. But I say unto you, that it shall be

more tolerable for the land of Sodom in the day of judgment, than for thee."

The worst sins are not committed in the sleazy atmosphere of taverns amid the raucous laughter of houses of ill-fame, or inside some garbage-ridden back alley where drugs are being sold. The worst sins are occurring in carpeted and air-conditioned church buildings where people hear the gospel, understand its value, but refuse to obey it. That is a sin against light. That is a sin against the provisional care of our Lord who is doing everything that is possible to woo lost mankind to himself. That is the reason that judgment must begin in the house of God.

Now, let us consider the highlights of the third chapter of Daniel, which of course is in reference to the fourth man in the furnace:

"He answered and said, lo, I see four men loose, walking in the midst of the fire, and they have no hurt; and the form of the fourth is like the Son of God"(3:25)

This is a grand manifestation of the Lord Jesus Christ. In theology, an Old Testament appearance of Jesus is called a "theophany." This is a theophany. Remember, Jesus is God. Wondrously, Jesus is as much God as though He were not man at all and He is as much man as though He were not God at all. He is not all God and no man; neither is He all man and no God. He is not half-God and half-man; He is the perfect God- man. Having established the deity of Christ as divine truth, it is easy to understand that His beginning was not in a manger in Bethlehem. Jesus has always been:

"In the beginning was the Word, and the Word was with God, and the Word was God. The same was in the beginning with God. All things were made by him; and without him was not anything made that was made" (John 1.-1~3).

In this passage that you have just read, verse one called Jesus "the Word" which comes from "logos," meaning "word, voice, utterance." To fully appreciate what I have just shared, note carefully Genesis 3:8:

"And they heard the voice of the Lord God walking in the garden in the cool of the day: and Adam and his wife hid themselves from the presence of the Lord God among the trees . of the garden."

Did you notice the word, "voice"? This can be accurately translated. "word," just as we have already seen in John 1:1. Amazingly, then, the first theophany, the first Old Testament appearance of the Lord Jesus Christ was in the Garden of Eden.

However, there are other appearances. I believe that Joshua met the Lord Jesus just before the entrance of the children of Israel into Canaan:

"And it came to pass, when Joshua was by Jericho, that he lifted up his eyes and looked and, behold, there stood a man over against him with his sword drawn in his hand; and Joshua went unto him, and said unto him, art thou for us, or for our adversaries? And he said. nay, but as captain of the host of the Lord am I now come. And Joshua fell on his face to the earth, and did worship, and said unto him, what saith my lord unto his servants? And the captain of the Lord's host said unto Joshua, Loose thy shoe from off thy foot; for the place whereon thou standest is holy. And Joshua did so "(Joshua 5:13-15).

I am quite sure that such dedicated young men as Shadrach, Meshach, and Abednego were well versed in the history of Christ's appearances among their forefathers. It had probably never crossed their minds, however, that they would one day have a face-to-face meeting with them like Adam or like Joshua. To stand in the presence of the beloved Christ and speak with Him about the burdens of the heart must have seemed like a dream from which they would never want to awake. But is was no dream, no vision! Jesus was with them! Jesus was there, actually there!

We should not forget the place where Christ was met by them. Nothing of a religious nature was taking place. There was no choir. There was no sermon that had been powerfully delivered. This was the most unlikely of places that one would expect to find Christ, particularly if the Christ that you envision is that of a lowly shepherd. Let there be no question about it! Jesus is the Good Shepherd, but that title reveals only a part of His character and personality. In totality, Jesus is the Lord of Glory! As such, He is also the Christ of every crisis and delights in surprising us with His presence at some of the most unexpected times.

It has been my observation by the accumulation of personal experiences that I have more often found Jesus in the routines of life with its mountains and valleys than in those times in which I have surrounded myself with the trappings of religion. Does this sound as though I am discouraging as unimportant our faithful support and attendance at worship services? Indeed not! Hebrews 10:25 declares simply:

"Not forsaking the assembling of ourselves together as the manner of some is, but exhorting one another and so much the 'more as ye see the day approaching."

What I am trying to say to you is that we should not allow ourselves to develop "tunnel vision" through which we can only meet Christ under certain specified conditions of our own making He cannot be contained, and He will not allow Himself to be restricted by the rigid concepts and creeds of His followers. Did He not advise us that His second coming would be at "such a day and hour as ye think not"?

One compliment must be paid Nebuchadnezzar. Whenever he was proven wrong, he quickly admitted it and tried to right the wrongs that he had caused others. You will remember the reward of elevation to a position of power that he gave Daniel in two. In much the same manner, he also made to Shadrach, Meshach, and Abednego:

"Therefore, I make a decree, that every people, nation, and language, who speak anything amiss against the God of Shadrach, Meshach and Abednego, shall be cut in pieces, and their houses shall be a dunghill, because there is no other God that can deliver alter this sort. Then the king promoted Shadrach, Meshach, and Abednego in the province of Babylon " (3:29-30)

Chapter 4

Nebuchadnezzar's Tree-Vision

In this chapter, we are allowed to pull back the curtain of the ages and view a most unusual incident in the life of the world's most powerful figure. It serves as a poignant lesson that no man rises so high in his own estimation and that of this world but that he can be brought low. God is not confined to the foolish restrictions of man's distorted self-values. Nebuchadnezzar had conquered his world but he had not conquered himself.

Babylon, sometimes called the Chaldean Empire, ruled the world from 625 to 538 B.C. Naboplassar (625-605 B.C.) was its founder. He represented the Chaldeans, a people whose home was on the Persian Gulf, and who gradually made themselves the masters of Babylon. At first a vassal king in Syria, Naboplassar revolted and became independent when troubles and misfortunes began in the Assyrian court. Later, he entered into an alliance with the Median king against his former friends in Assyria. Through the overthrow of Nineveh, the capital city of Assyria, and the break-up of the Assyrian Empire, the Babylonian state received large areas of territory. For a short time thereafter, Babylon filled a great place in history.

Naboplassar was followed by his renowned son Nebuchadnezzar (605-561 B.C.), whose gigantic architectural works, of which we have already spoken, rendered Babylon the wonder of the ancient world.

Jerusalem, after revolting, was taken and sacked. Nebuchadnezzar stripped the temple of its sacred vessels of silver and gold, which were carried away to Babylon, and the temple itself was given to flames.

With Jerusalem, subdued, Nebuchadnezzar pushed with all of his forces the siege that he had laid around the city of Tyre, which siege had been started several years before. In biblical times, it was not unusual for an army to completely a city, thereby cutting off its food and water supplies, stay there until the city was literally starved out. But, after years, the city fell. Ezekiel says of those days:

"Son of man, Nebuchadnezzar, king of Babylon. Caused his army to serve a great service against Tyrus: every head was made bald, and every shoulder was peeled: yet he had no wages, not his army, for Cyrus, for the service that he had served against it. Therefore thus saith the Lord God; behold I will give the land of Egypt unto Nebuchadnezzar king of Babylon; and he shall take her multitude, and take her spoil, and take her prey; and it shall be the wages for his army" (Ezekiel 29:18-19).

Nebuchadnezzar defeated Tyre, but in the process of doing so, suffered heavy financial losses. Since Tyre was a coastal , they placed all their treasures on ship and sent them away. As a result, when the city finally fell, there was nothing of value is spoils of victory to replenish the war chest of Nebuchadnezzar. Needing money, as Ezekiel indicated in the verses just quoted, Nebuchadnezzar took his army into Egypt and took spoils from his invasion there.

Returning to Babylon, he began the massive architectural and building projects for which he is best remembered by the historian. One of his inscriptions that has been unearthed reads, "Like dear life, love I the building of their lodging places." He was speaking of his obsession with the construction and the beautification of religious buildings and shrines.

One of the marvels of the ancient world was the complex built by Nebuchadnezzar in Babylon called "The Hanging Gardens," to which we have previously alluded in this study. Perhaps it was while he was strolling among its many trees one night that this vision in chapter four came to him in complete form. Quite likely his evening had begun rather uneventfully as many others of his evenings had done. Maybe there had been one of his customary state dinners that he had attended. Merriment and good conversation had abounded. Returning to his palace, he may have dropped off to sleep with pleasant thoughts flooding his mind. But then, unexpectedly, a panorama of images begins racing through the corridors of his unconsciousness. Perhaps he awakened and decided that the cool air would be a refreshing tonic:

"I Nebuchadnezzar was at rest in mine house. and flourishing in my palace; I saw a dream which made me afraid, and the thoughts upon my bed and the visions of my head troubled me"(4.'4-5).

Whatever the case, whether he stayed among the covers of his royal bed for the entire restless night, or whether he walked it off until the rising of the sun, one thing is certain, his dream had a definite impact upon him that he could not simply shrug off.

This chapter serves as an international, world-wide declaration by the king. Obviously, the significance of his dream was more than that of a common nightmare. Nebuchadnezzar believed that the entire population of the world could be benefited by this personal word from the Lord. That is the reason that verse one says:

"Nebuchadnezzar the king. unto all people, nations, and languages, that dwell in all the earth, peace be multiplied unto you.

Verse two and three give us a praise statement that fell from the lips of this pagan king. If you will read carefully the words that he said, you will find that it is the kind of adoration that we would ordinarily associate with only the saints of God:

"I thought it good to show the signs and wonders that the high God hath wrought toward me. How great are his signs! How mighty are his wonders! His kingdom is an everlasting kingdom! His dominion is from generation to generation!"

In these verses, our God is presented as being:

(1) SENSITIVE: ". . . the high God hath wrought toward me . . ." Unlike the gods of heathenism, Jehovah cares for the individual. Nebuchadnezzar had found that the Lord was a personal God.

(2) STRONG: "How great are his signs . . ." The Lord had used signs that could not be duplicated by the human mind or muscle. Nebuchadnezzar had seen it all! The most advanced of military design and strategy had been used against him, yet we find him here speaking of the greatness of God's signs.

(3) SUPERNATURAL: "How marvelous are his wonders!" Remember, the man uttering these words had supervised the construction of massive building projects.

He was, nevertheless, awed by the omnipotent power of God in the creation of everything that exits.

(4) SOVEREIGN: "His kingdom is an everlasting kingdom!" The king recognized a fundamental difference between the kingdom of Babylon and the kingdom of God. Babylon would one day fall; the kingdom of God would never end.

(5) SECURE: "His dominion is from generation to generation!" Undoubtedly, because of the rise and fall of ancient royal families, Nebuchadnezzar must have feared whether he would even have a kingdom to leave as an inheritance to his sons. God's kingdom will endure for the benefit of all those who especially crave its graces.

As we move to verses four and five, an experience that is common befalls the king. He is at rest. He is enjoying himself:

"I Nebuchadnezzar was at rest in mine house. And flourishing in my palace; I saw a dream which made me afraid, and the thoughts upon my bed and. the visions of my head troubled me. "

Is it not a fact of life, particularly for those of us who trust Christ, that following a great victory we are besieged with problems? Here was Nebuchadnezzar in his place, away from the rigors of the battlefield. Suddenly, his relaxation is shattered by a vision so awful that he cannot rest.

So, what does he do? In spite of the fact that men who dabble in the spirit-world of the occult had previously proven themselves inept and unable to decipher dreams and visions (see chapter one), he calls upon them again:

"Therefore made I a decree to bring in all the wise men of Babylon before me, that they might make known unto me the interpretation of the dream. Then came in the magicians. The astrologers, the Chaldeans. and the soothsayers: and I told the dream before them; but they did not make known unto me the interpretation thereof' (4:6- 7).

Do not be unduly harsh on the wisdom of the king for resorting to past methods that had already failed him. Most people that I know, including those I esteem as some of God's choicest saints, occasionally fall into sin. With sincere determination we make vows that we will never yield to that same temptation again. But, guess what, we do! Not only will we commit it again; but we will commit it again and again and again. Like Paul, our spirit within us screams:

"For that which I do I allow not. for what would, that do I not; but what I hate, that do I. . . 0 wretched man that I am! Who shall deliver me from the body of this death? I thank God through Jesus Christ our Lord. So then with the mind I myself serve the law of God; but with the flesh the law of sin "(Romans 7:15. 24-25).

As expected, the magicians, soothsayers, astrologers, and Chaldeans were unable to interpret the vision of Nebuchadnezzar. As before, noble Daniel was called upon to aid the king.

I see a beautiful quality about Daniel that is shared by the king as he addressed this faithful man of God. Daniel gave evidence that he was thoroughly motivated by the able to recognize not only that Daniel was different, but he was different! Listen to the king's words of admiration respect:

"But at last Daniel came in before me, whose name was Belteshazzar, according to the name of my god, AND IN WHOM IS THE SPIRIT OF THE HOL Y GODS: and before him I told the dream. saying, O Belteshazzar, master of the magicians, because I KNOW THE SPIRIT OF THE HOL Y GODS IS IN THEE, and no secret troubleth thee, tell me the , visions of m y dream that I have seen, and the interpretations ' ' thereof. . . This dream I king Nebuchadnezzar have seen. Now than, 0 Belteshazzar, declare the interpretation thereof,' forasmuch as all the wise men of my kingdom are not able to make known unto me the interpretation: but thou art able; FOR THE SPIRIT OF THE HOLY GODS IS IN THEE" (4:8-9. I 8). .

Outward confession of God by those who follow Him is the trademark of a victorious faith. The bloody pages of Christian history are testimony enough of the fact that true faith in Jesus will not beget a silent disciple. Ours has always been a commission by the Lord to confess Him openly. The world readily recognizes genuine Christian character and just as readily can perceive that which is phony. The blight of the church in our modem day is that her ranks are filled with those who sing loudly, "Like a Mighty Army Moves The Church of God," when they, themselves, are so timid each day with an open acknowledgement of their faith as to render it virtually imperceptible by those with whom they come in contact. No individual in the Scriptures who" attained even the nodding approval of God ever left a question mark in the mind of anyone about where they stood with the Lord. Such was the case with Daniel.

With confident expectation in God's willingness to provide him with divine knowledge in any situation, Daniel came before the king. Nebuchadnezzar began his recitation of the vision:

"Thus were the visions of mine head in my bed; I saw, and behold a tree in the midst of the earth, and the height thereof was great. The tree grew, and was strong, and the height thereof reached unto heaven, and the sight thereof to the end of all the earth: the leaves thereof were fair. and the fruit thereof much, and in it was meat for all: the beasts of the field had shadow under it. and the fowls of the heaven dwelt in the boughs thereof and all flesh was fed of it"(4.-10-12).

Before we continue with the entire vision, let us read the interpretation of Daniel for this opening part:

"The tree that thou sawest, which grew, and was strong, whose height reached unto the heaven, and the sight thereof to all the earth; whose leaves were fair, and the fruit thereof much, and in it was meat for all; under which the beasts of the field dwelt; and upon whose branches the fowls of the heaven had their habitation; it is thou, O king, that art grown and become strong. for thy greatness is grown, and reacheth unto heaven, and thy dominion to the end of the earth" (4.-20-21).

Obviously, the primary symbolism of the tree concerns the greatness and the grandeur of the Babylonian Empire, but there is a secondary meaning that is of far greater significance than the first. In Revelation, Babylon is used as a picture of the false church of the end-time. Read Revelation 18:1-2:

"And after these things I saw another angel come down from heaven, having great power; and the earth was lightened with his glory. And he cried mightily with a strong voice, saying. Babylon the great is fallen, and is become the

habitation of devils, and the hold of every foul spirit, and a cage of every unclean and hateful bird".

If you will study the seventeenth chapter of Revelation, you will learn that this world is headed for a convulsive upheaval as the antichrist and his henchmen (the ten-nation federation) turn one against the other until Babylon (the false religious-economic system) stands in ruin. The very name "Babylon" means "confusion." And in the final throes of her that word is particularly appropriate in application to the world disorder that will follow the death of the Roman and religious influence.

But the fall of the organized structure does not mean the of demonic influences. By studying Revelation 18:2, we observe that the false apostate church of the antichrist at the end-time will be a :

HABITATION OF DEMONS: For any person who ever uncovered a den of snakes, there is an indelible mark of experience left on his mind. It is as though that den is the point of origin for all the snakes of the world. Huge balls of squirming serpents are everywhere. Just like a physical den of vipers spiritual Babylon will become the home of the demons.

(2) HOLD OF FOUL SPIRITS: The spirits of licentiousness, of malice, of evil thinking, of every device used by Satan to bind and shackle the people of this world will find in spiritual Babylon a stronghold in which to dwell.

(3) HAVEN OF UNCLEAN AND HATEFUL BIRDS: The term, "birds," seems somewhat out of place here. We do not ordinarily associate birds with the likes of demons and evil spirits. It must be clearly understood that these are not beautiful, multi-colored songbirds; instead, they are vultures, sitting patiently on the limbs of liberalism in the false church and silently waiting to pick the carcasses of those who will be so foolish as to come under the deadening influence of spiritual Babylon. Jesus spoke of these "birds" in His parable of the mustard seed in Matthew 13:31-32:

"Another parable put he forth unto them, saying, the kingdom of heaven is like to a grain of mustard seed. which a man took, and sowed in his field; which indeed is the least of all the seeds, but when it is grown, it is the greatest among

herbs, and becometh a tree. so that the birds of the air come and lodge in the branches thereof"

Often this parable is interpreted as a picture of what happens when a little seed is received into a man's heart. That little seed begins to grow, according to this interpretation, until it becomes a big beautiful tree of faith in which can be found the songbirds of faith. However, this is totally incorrect because this interpretation does not harmonize with the other parables of the kingdom found in the same chapter. The other parables speak of the conflicts of the devil that are present in all those who have aspirations to be a part of the kingdom's work. Therefore, for the sake of context, the parable of the mustard seed must in some way show the threat of Satan's attempts to thwart God's plans.

First, by common sense, we see that the tree sprang from the herb. Please note. Trees and herbs are two entirely different plants. As a consequence, it would only be by a supernatural monstrosity of the worst sort that trees could grow from herbs. This parable, then, is describing the simplicity of the faithful early church that will eventually be replaced by the world-wide church of the end-time. As such, the vultures of hell find a place within a corrupt church to lodge. Why are they there? Look at the parable of the sower in Matthew 13:4:

"And when he sowed, some seeds fell by the way side. and the fowls came and devoured them up. "

What are these fowls? By the very words of Jesus, We find that these are demon-creatures. Matthew 13-19 says of them:

"When any one heareth the word of the kingdom, and understandeth it not, then cometh the wicked one, and catcheth away that which was sown in his heart. This is he which receiveth seed by the way side. "

So, now it is clear! Spiritual Babylon, the wicked apostate church and economic system of the antichrist, will the home of liberal theology where these demon vultures will live. Every person reading this book can name other people who accepted the seed of the gospel, were saved, then came under the influence of a liberal church, finally becoming a social-minded Christian with none of the virtues of the saint. Is it not sad that the worst enemies of the new believer are those who claim to be saved but still reject all or part of the Bible.

To tie all this together, remember our starting point in the prophecies of Daniel and his interpretation of Nebuchadnezzar's tree-vision in the fourth chapter of the Book of Daniel. There is a continual similarity between his words and those of Jesus in the thirteen chapter of Matthew and those of John in the eighteenth chapter of Revelation.

You will recall that the kingdom of Babylon was the first of the world empires. It is that literal nation that God chooses to use as a reference point for describing the decadent condition of this world system of the end-time. She will rule the world of the tribulation period. It cannot be accurately understood, by those of us who are fortunate enough to be saved and living prior to that awful time, how grim this universal evil influence will be in the false end-time church so dominated by the ugly birds of demonic liberalism.

Again, as I have shared before, to accurately interpret prophecies in the Scriptures, you must recognize the use of a technique employed frequently in the Bible known as "prophecy of double reference." Prophecy of double reference means predicting the occurrence of a soon-coming event through which we can see a farther, more important event. In this instance, Nebuchadnezzar's wicked influence and God's divine affliction upon him, was the soon-coming event through which Daniel tried to show the farther event of the ungodly antichrist and his demise at the hand of the Almighty.

So, swinging back from the far event of the apostate church in the eighteenth chapter of Revelation, we are given the nearer interpretation of the tree vision in Daniel 4:22-23.

"It is thou, O king, that art grown and become strong: for thy greatness is grown, and reacheth unto heaven, and thy dominion to the end of the earth. And whereas the king saw a watcher and an holy one coming down from heaven, and saying, hew the tree down, and destroy it; yet lea ye the stump of the roots thereof in the earth. even with a band of iron and brass, in the tender grass of the field; and let it be wet with the dew of heaven, and let his portion be with the beasts of the field, till seven times pass over him. "

No sane man should ever allow himself the luxury of slipping into the egotistical presumption that his personal greatness is too high for even God to hurdle. This verse clearly reminds us that the very God of heaven is totally aware of man's estimation of himself and is perfectly capable of hewing that man down at the time of heaven's choosing. Such was the case with Nebuchadnezzar and his vast empire.

The Almighty King came to the earthly plane of this world and met the monarch of Babylon on his own level. Our Lord's instructions were swift and His orders equally chilling as He dictated His dealings with the nation and with its ruler. First, the nation was to be hewn down, leaving only the stump. From that stump will eventually emerge the last days' false church and economic system. Second, Nebuchadnezzar was told that he would be banished to the fields, there to dwell among the animals until "seven times" should pass over him. "Times" is an archaic expression for years. Therefore, the king's warning meant that he was destined to live as an animal. What a fall from a place of prominence in the palace to debasement in the fields.

What would happen to his nation while Nebuchadnezzar was suffering the punishment of the Lord? What, or who, would keep it safe from invading marauders or ambitious politicians? Surely these disturbing thoughts riveted the troubled mind of the king. The iron and brass bands commanded by the Lord to be placed around the stump were to protect the king's interest until he had served his divine sentence:

"And whereas they commanded to leave the stump of the tree roots; thy kingdom shall be sure unto thee, after that thou shalt have known that the heavens do rule"(4:26).

Daniel concluded his interpretation of the tree vision by the king to reverse himself in his attempts to the accomplishments of his own making rather than the deeds of God. Read verse 27:

"Wherefore, O king, let my counsel be acceptable unto thee. and break 017' thy sins by righteousness, and thine iniquities by shewing mercy to the poor," if it may be a lengthening of the tranquility."

Good counseling for anybody suffering under the pressure can be found here. Our emotional health, as well as our health, is dependent upon two relationships-—our with God and our fellowship with the other members of the human race:

(1) WITH GOD: "... *Break off thy sins by righteousness...* " This reflects the necessity of maintaining a sturdy union with the Father. We are not only exhorted to "*break off our sins* "-- that would be mere reformation. No, we are exhorted to "*break off our sins BY RIGHTEOUSNESS* "—-that is regeneration. The individual who simply ceases to sin is not really right with God. Sins have not been completely eradicated and forgiven from the believer's divine record until the righteousness of God has cleansed him. Romans 10:4 says, "*For Christ is the end of the law for righteousness to every one that believeth.* "

(2) WITH MAN: *. . and thine iniquities by shewing mercy to the poor. . .* " It is common knowledge to the worldly that the church of the Lord Jesus Christ preaches a good case for the unfortunate but actually does little that expresses genuine compassion. I do not believe that this verse is primarily instructing the saint to be more active in charitable contributions of money. Such may be 'included in this exhortation by Daniel, but because of the context in which the phrase is found I am more given to the idea that mercy meant the releasing of the poor from harsh bondage in order that they might enjoy the necessary freedom to live a more productive life.

Freedom, true freedom, can only come through Jesus Christ. The bondage of the heart and soul binds a man more tightly than the chains of iron. The real hunger of every hum an being on the face of this planet is the hunger of the spirit for a union with God. Until a believer finds himself in a daily routine of witness for Christ, he cannot be one who is merciful to the poor, regardless of the size of his donations to benevolent causes.

These two relationships, those with God and with man. Are absolutely essential for a person to have a "... *lengthening of thy tranquility.* " Thousands of dollars could be saved by distraught individuals in the purchases of medical mood-levelers and psychiatric services if they would only learn that a peaceful mind comes from a correct vertical relationship with God and a correct horizontal relationship with man.

What happened? Did the king suffer as Daniel had said?

"All this came upon the king Nebuchadnezzar. At the end of twelve months he walked in the palace of the kingdom of Babylon. The king spake, and said. is not this great Babylon. that I have built for the house of the kingdom by the might of my power, and for the honour of my majesty?" (4:28-30).

Proud Nebuchadnezzar! Note that God gave him plenty of time to repent! But that should not strike us unusual. God always has given the most flagrant of sinners a space of time to repent. It is a part of the divine character of the Almighty to do so:

The Lard is not slack concerning his promises. As some men count slackness; but is longsuffering to us-ward. Not willing that any should perish. but that all should come to repentance (II Peter 3:9).

You and I do not possess the infinite mercy of our Father who is able to endure the puny insults of man without immediately responding in vengeance. It is just a plain Bible fact that God desires fellowship with even the grossest of sinners. Included among those God patiently waited upon was Nebuchadnezzar, a pagan king. For twelve months, one whole year, this proud was allowed ample time to confess his sins.

Probably, in those first few weeks immediately following interpretation of the vision, he was nervously agitated, frightened. But since no harm came as days melted into the king most likely settled back into his previous The entire episode was accepted as nothing more than incidental disturbance that required no continuing measures the actual occurrence of the prophet's dread warning. is always so with the bent characteristic of man's twisted that he will continue to perpetuate his favorite sin with teal concern as long as no judgment seems headed his way. is in exact conformity with the writer of Ecclesiastes who said:

"Because sentence against an evil work is not executed speedily, therefore the heart of sons of men is fully set in them to do evil" (Ecclesiastes 8:11).

Nebuchadnezzar did not heed! His warning was given! A stay of punishment was granted from the divine jurisdiction of heaven! But in spite of the lingering patience and mercy of God, he procrastinated, he waited, somehow convincing himself, there was no cause to worry. For twelve long months he carried on his business in the kingdom as usual. For twelve long months he hardened his heart! For twelve long months he pursued the fanciful dreams and ambitions of his life! Finally, God's mercy wore thin, and all of the king's wall of judgment crumbled to his feet. Like the somber notes of the midnight bell, God's words, through the prophet from the year before, began bringing the heavy hammer of chastisement upon the head of Nebuchadnezzar:

"While the word was in the king 's mouth, there fell a voice from heaven, saying, O king Nebuchadnezzar, to thee it is spoken, the kingdom is departed from thee. And they shall drive thee from men, and thy dwelling shall be with the beasts of the field: they shall make thee to eat grass as oxen, and seven times shall pass over thee, until thou know that the Most High ruleth in the kingdom of men, and giveth it to whom so ever he will. The some hour was the thing fulfilled upon Nebuchadnezzar? and he was driven from men, and did eat grass as oxen, and his body was wet with the dew of heaven, till his hairs were grown like eagles' feathers, and his nails like birds' claws" (4:31-33).

This lofty ancient monarch fell from the royal position of pomp and circumstance to the lowly estate of a common animal in a pasture. Babylon was noted for its equivalent of our modern-day zoo, bringing a menagerie of unusual and exotic animals from throughout the world. With the manifestation of animal symptoms, it may well have been that his closest advisors felt it best to place him in one of these magnificently kept royal gardens.

In our day, we are able to recognize this strange affliction as boanthropy. Boanthropy is an emotional disorder in which its victim sees himself as a particular animal and begins to develop patterns of behavior normally associated with that
animal.

Can you imagine the rumors that were whispered about the province? All sorts of questions about the nation's leadership had to be resolved. Was this a temporary mental malady, or was the king permanently disabled? Should someone be selected to serve as interim in his absence, or should a new ruler be crowned?

I think that I would be remiss if I did not make you aware of a message that goes beyond this segment in an ancient king's life. Paul shares an interesting principle in I Corinthians 2:14 when he says:

"But the natural man receiveth not the things of the Spirit of God: for they are foolishness unto him; neither can he know them, because they are spiritually discerned."

One translation renders "natural man" as "animal man." He is a man who, like an animal, lives only for the satisfaction of basic appetites, like food and water and sex. The animal man has little time for the considering of eternal truths. He is a word used for "flesh" or "meat." You have seen word in other descriptive words (i.e. "carnivorous animal" a flesh-eating animal). The unspiritual man is carnivorous; he is carnal. Though he would never see it in himself, he conducts his affairs with the same view to this world as an animal.

Nebuchadnezzar was just such a man. He was carnal; he was animal in his ambitions and passions. The horrible sight of a mud-caked king wallowing in the fields with his nails like and his hair like feathers is a vivid picture of how God the carnal individual who may be well-groomed, charming, and personable outwardly. God sees his heart and knows that at man is nothing more than a brute beast inside. Dear Reader, examine yourself. Honestly open your heart and allow the illuminating presence of God's. Spirit to examine it.

As unfortunate as this incident was in the life of the king, it did bring happy results. Sometimes a crushing problem with no apparent solution is the only way that God can penetrate the mind and heart of a wayward person:

"And at the end of the days I Nebuchadnezzar lifted up mine eyes unto heaven, and mine understanding returned unto me, ' and I blessed the Most High, and I praised and honored him that liveth forever, whose dominion is an everlasting dominion, and his kingdom is from generation to generation. And all the inhabitants of the earth are reputed as nothing, and he doeth according to his will in the army of heaven; and among the inhabitants of the earth; and none can stay his hand, or say unto him what doest thou? At the same time my reason returned

unto me, and for the glory of my kingdom, mine honour and brightness returned unto me; and my counselors and my lords sought unto me. Now I Nebuchadnezzar praise and extol and honor the King of heaven, all whose works are truth, and his ways judgment: and those that walk in pride he is able to debase" (4:34-37).

Was Nebuchadnezzar saved? This is a question that Bible commentators have difficulty answering. The honest truth of the matter is that we just do not know. These verses sound like words that could only come from the lips of a man who is yielded to the Lord, but they may have been nothing more than "foxhole religion."

This was not the first time that the king sounded like a man of God. Remember his words in Daniel 2:47:

"The king answered unto Daniel, and said, of a truth it is, that your God is a God of gods, and a Lord of kings, and a revealer of secrets, seeing thou couldest reveal this secret. "

But alter making such a tremendous confession, he exalted himself above God. Perhaps that was what he was doing again after the episode of his exile.

Was Nebuchadnezzar saved? We just do not know. More important, are you?

II

Chapter five

Handwriting On The Wall

We find ourselves having arrived, in our study of the Book Daniel, at one of the most intriguing stories in the entire Word of God. It is not an excerpt from ancient fiction. It is not exaggeration of an actual occurrence that has been dramatized literature to prove a religious point. This incident happened as it was recorded by the prophet. Granted, for centuries narrative was the object of the critics' scorn; but secular discoveries have all but disqualified the challenges these ignorant skeptics and reduced their learned protestations to the level of mere babbling.

Take, as an example, the promise of King Belshazzar found in verse 16. His commitment to Daniel was that he (Daniel) would be made the third ruler in Babylon if he could 'successfully decipher the handwriting on the wall. How could this be? Pompous historians strutted their ridicule of the 'Scriptures by asserting that no accounts of a king in Babylon by the name of Belshazzar could even be found. All sorts of stinging verbal barbs were aimed by these intellectuals toward the Bible-honoring church.

All that the faithful believer could say in response to these cruel cuts was that God's Word was somehow true in this particular matter as it is also true in all others. There seemed to be no other answer. The critics were right in their assertion that only the Bible mentioned Belshazzar. Reliable documents of that ancient day contained no reference of him, but instead, they consistently referred to the king of Babylon during that period as Nabonidus.

Well, for generations there was nothing to support the scriptural account until one fateful day an archaeological discovery produced ancient authentication of a co-regent in Babylon by the name of "Bel-shar-uzzar." This Bel-shar-uzzar was the Belshazzar of the Bible. It was revealed of him that he was the grandson of Nebuchadnezzar. His father was the son of Nebuchadnezzar, and his name was Nabonidus of whom secular history speaks.

Nabonidus had been a conquering general in his father's army. It was only fitting that when Nebuchadnezzar died. His kingdom was passed to Nabonidus. But Nabonidus showed no fondness for the administration of the government. He loved the outdoor life. Soon after assuming control of the empire, he began taking long hunting trips. These safaris claimed much of his time and energy. The affairs of state were left lacking a leader.

To rectify this problem. Nabonidus turned to his son, Belshazzar. He made his son the second ruler in the kingdom; he was a co-regent, a viceroy, to his father, Nabonidus. Therefore, the Scriptures were proven to be historically accurate in the promise of Belshazzar to make Daniel the third ruler in the kingdom. Always remember that while the Bible is not primarily a book of science or history, if it is indeed the Word of God, it must be totally correct when making statements that pertain to science and history. Such was the case in the question of Belshazzar in Babylon.

To set the stage for the memorable evening depicted in this fifth chapter, I think we can resort to some imagination of what it may have been like to attend this gala feast in the banquet hall of the king. As has been true throughout the centuries, much drinking was the order of the day at this party in the same way that alcohol has been in parties and social gatherings innumerable. Note the references to drinking in these opening verses:

"Belshazzar the king made a great feast to a thousand of his lords, and DRANK wine be/ore the thousand. Belshazzar, whiles he TASTED the wine, commanded to bring the golden and silver vessels which his father Nebuchadnezzar had taken out of the temple which was in Jerusalem; that the king, and his princes, his wives, and his concubines, might DRINK therein. Then they brought the golden vessels that were taken out of the house of God which was at Jerusalem; and the king, and his princes, his wives, and his concubines, DRANK in them. They DRANK wine, and praised the gods of gold, and of silver, of brass, of iron, of wood, and of stone" (5:1-4).

All was festive! The night was a night to remember! The wealthy, the aristocratic, the powerful, arrived in their finest and most glittering garments. Dashing were the gentlemen and exquisite were the ladies. As lord after lord, and lady after lady, entered the banquet hall, the sound of oohs and ahs wafted like waves across the crowd as they were thrilled by the presence of the mighty and of the famous.

Elegantly-designed candelabras glimmered in the hall, lighting the entire area with an atmosphere of soft and warm romance. Exotic foods were piled in mounds upon colorfully decorated tables that strained beneath their delicious burdens. Here and there were male and female servants carrying the choicest of wines to refill the drained cups and goblets of the revellers.

Because the Babylonians loved music (See Daniel 3:5), we know that minstrels and musicians of every kind could be seen winding their ways through the crowd as they lightly played upon the instruments of their specialty. Wine and song! What a pleasing combination!

Only one thing was lacking for the entertainment to be complete. Such a sensual, pleasure-ridden gathering needed the ultimate in sensuality! Soon, the scantily-clad bodies of the kingdom's most attractive girls were swirling before the lustful eyes of the lords. An occasional hand would reach upward from a couch made of cushions in a vain effort to pull one of the women down to him. Failing, that same hand would reach for a full goblet and pour out its contents into an open mouth.

As the evening wore on, the most blatant of orgy activities finally began to fail to excite the passions of the drunkened assemblage. It was then that Belshazzar, whose courage was falsely bolstered by drink, made a fool's mistake and called for the vessels of the temple that had been taken from God's house in Jerusalem by his grandfather, Nebuchadnezzar. Whispering to an attendant, the order was given. Off to their royal museum they ran, soon returning with the sanctified vessels of the Lord.

Mocking the God Jehovah, Belshazzar ordered the vessels distributed among the throng. Only heaven knows the anger that boiled within the heart of God as He watched men laugh and desecrate the holy things of His own making. But heaven was not on the mind of Belshazzar as he lifted a temple cup and poured crimson wine from it into his parted lips and allowed it to trickle down his beard and onto his royal vestments.

Suddenly, right in the midst of his unbridled merriment, an attendant touched his arm and directed the king's attention to a nearby wall. With another cup halfway to his lips, his hand stopped, suspended in midair. The redness in his cheeks turned ashen white and his smile turned to a frown of fear:

"In the same hour came forth fingers of a man's hand. And wrote over against the candlestick upon the plaster of the wall of the king': palace: and the king saw the part of the hand that wrote. Then the king': countenance changed, and his thoughts troubled him, so that the joints of his loins were loosed, and his knees smote one against another" (5:5-6).

The laughter subsided. The dancing girls grew still; aware of their nakedness they began reaching for something to use as a covering. Seasoned military men uneasily gripped the swords at their sides, nervously looking quickly around them for an enemy. At the royal head table, the king was in panic, his heart pounding, his knees jerking uncontrollably.

As Nebuchadnezzar had done before him, Belshazzar "*cried aloud*" for the Chaldeans, the astrologers, and the soothsayers. In they came as the sea of people parted to allow them entrance. They looked, they peered, they scrutinized, and they examined; but nothing could be made of the strange words on the wall. Fear mounted in the king's heart. His wisest and most knowledgeable men in the kingdom had failed him.

"Then was king Belshazzar greatly troubled, and his countenance was changed in him, and his lords were astonied" (5:9).

"Astonied" is a stronger word than our modern word, "astonished." To be astonied was to be stricken with a situation that was unbelievable. That word alone establishes the paralyzing atmosphere that prevailed.

One can only wonder what Belshazzar's next move might been had it not been for the entrance of the queen. Though is no indication that this woman knew the Lord, she did the presence of God in the prophet's life:

"Now the queen by reason of the words of the king and his lords came into the banquet house: and the queen spake and said. O king, live forever; let not thy thoughts trouble thee, nor let thy countenance be changed. There is a man in

thy kingdom. IN WHOM IS THE SPIRIT OF THE HOLY GODS: and in the days of thy father LIGHT AND UNDERSTANDING AND WISDOM. LIKE THE WISDOM OF THE GODS. WAS FOUND IN HIM; whom the king Nebuchadnezzar thy father the king, I say, thy father, made master of the magicians, astrologers, Chaldeans, and soothsayers; forasmuch' as AN EXCELLENT SPIRIT and knowledge. and understanding, interpreting qfdrearns, and shewing of hard sentences, and dissolving of doubts, were FOUND IN THE SAME DANIEL. whom the king named Belteshazzar: now let Daniel be called, and he will shew the interpretation " (5:10-l2).

Man rides in planes instead of camel-back, he may wear suits and ties instead of robes and turbans, but he still thinks, acts, and reacts in the same ageless way. He has no time or need for God during the happy days of his life. Sincere people of God are either ignored or used for the butt end of cruel jokes and taunts. The philosophy of hell, "eat, drink, and be merry," is the order of man's foolish days. But let him be stricken with a grave problem so severe that the best minds of this world can provide no answer, and man is forced to turn to God and to the people of God whom he had previously scorned.

A man settles in his easy chair with the Sunday comics and a cup of coffee while his patient wife scurries out with the children to church services. Sunday School is fine for women and children, but not for real men. He will watch football gamed on his remote control television set throughout the Lord's Day until his eyes are as big as coconuts and his brain the size of a pea. Weekdays, after work, finds him stopping for a drink with the good old boys at his favorite happy hour.

One day, strangely sick with unusual symptoms. He staggers to his doctor's office, there to hear the horrible news that very soon he will die. Frantically. he pleads for his doctor to do something, anything. There is no known cure. There is no treatment. There is no hope. Soon, he will die. It will all be over.

When that man leaves his doctor's office. where does he go? Does he hurry to happy hour? Does he beat it to the stadium to buy his discount tickets for next week's big game? No, with his lower lip quivering in fear and his hands trembling so violently that he can scarcely hold the steering wheel, he drives home. His face wet with perspiration and tears, he sobs for his shocked wife to "call the Reverend."

Belshazzar was faced with the same awful dilemma. His worst nightmare was a reality. What had brought the king to this position of a panicky potentate?

There are some sins that God will patiently endure. No sin will be overlooked. If ever one-half of one sin goes unpunished, God will topple from His throne of holiness. But some sins will not invoke the judgment of the Lord with the same rapidity as will others.

As the wine flowed through the banquet hall, making its partakers so intoxicated that normal inhibitions of decency gave way to unimaginable filth, God sat quietly on His throne. As the dancing girls immodestly fired the animal passions of their audience into flaming lusts, God scarcely moved. But when the holy vessels of God were jeered, abused, and misused, the wrath of the Almighty exploded.

The nearness of personal or national destruction can be predicted by the attitude of that person or nation toward the holy, sanctified things of God. God will not suffer long the challenges of ungodly men to go unanswered.

My deepest concern for America is that it is no longer the country I knew as a lad. Where the name of God was once welcomed and revered in education, government, and society, it is now ignored, attacked, and vilified! A nation's security before God is established by which topics are used for its humor. Talk shows, situation comedies, and the music industry echo with ribald laughter as blasphemous anecdotes and humor belched from the pit of hell are the main course delivered to a nation. One of three things are on our country's horizon: revival, ruin, or the return of Christ.

So, Daniel is ordered brought before the king. Perhaps it after midnight when the prophet was awakened by a loud at his door. Opening the door just a crack and peering the darkness, he could distinguish under the torch light a of elegantly dressed, but disheveled, men. Hands reached for him, pulling him helter-skelter down the streets and around the corners until he arrived at the area just in front of the grand banquet hall, where frightened men and women were hastily exiting and retreating into the darkness.

Entering the main entrance, Daniel probably perceived a somber mood hanging like a thick cloud. A large crowd was still inside the hall, whispering to one another with hushed tones. Little, tightly-knit clusters were making hand motions as they talked with frenzied animation. To the front Daniel strode until he was directly before the king, who with obvious agitation, swept his hand toward the writing on the wall while he quickly told the prophet of the unsettling events that had just transpired. His promises of reward tumbled from his lips with a note of begging, like a child in danger of a whipping, pleading and bargaining with his father not to do so.

Oh, I am so thankful for a man like Daniel. I have been privileged to meet a few. Look at his response to the king:

"Then Daniel answered and said before the king, let thy gifts be to thyself and give thy rewards to another; yet I will read the unto the king, and make known to him the interpretation "(5:17)

He could not be bought! His message was not subject to bartering! Prestige before his peers mounted for little in comparison to the approving look of the Almighty. Paul expressed this same feeling in I Thessalonians 2:4:

"But as we were allowed of God to be put in trust with the gospel. even so we speak; not as pleasing men, but God, which trieth our hearts"

Great men recognize the value of their causes. Men like Daniel and Paul would choose the displeasure of kings over the criticism of God. To them, there was no choice! Their minds and hearts were already fixed to serve the Lord, whatever the cost!

In Daniel 9:18-21, the prophet reminds Belshazzar of his grandfather Nebuchadnezzar's humiliation. God's severe dealings with the world's most powerful man had been the result of his pride:

"But when his heart was lifted up, and his mind hardened in pride. he was deposed from his kingly throne, and they took his glory from him: and he was driven from the sons of men; and his heart was made like the beasts, and his

dwelling was with the wild asses: they fed him with grass like oxen, and his body was wet with the dew of heaven; till he knew that the most high God ruled in the kingdom of men, and that he appointeth over it whomsoever he will."

God hates pride! Judgment will inevitably fall upon the man who haughtily places himself higher than he ought. God hates pride! Pride smacks of an independent spirit that refuses to honor God or man. One strong wanting is given in Proverbs 6:16-17:

"These six things doth the Lord hate: yea, seven are an abomination to him: a proud look, a lying tongue. and hands that shed innocent blood, an heart that deviseth wicked imaginations, feet that be swift in running to mischief: a false witness that speaketh lies, and he that soweth discord among brethren. "

An example of God's hatred of pride can be seen in His reason for the destruction of Sodom and Gommorah. Contrary to popular belief, these ancient people were not destroyed because of their ugly practice of homosexuality. To discover the real reason for their annihilation, read the following verses and note their pride:

"As I live, saith the Lord God, Sodom thy sister hath not done, she nor her sisters, as thou hast done, thou and thy daughters. Behold, this was the iniquity of thy sister Sodom, pride, fullness of bread. and abundance of idleness was in her and in her daughters, neither did she strengthen the hand of the poor and needy. And they were haughty. and committed abomination before me; therefore, I took them away as I saw good " (Ezekiel 16:48-50).

Daniel, being the man of God and student of the Word that he was, was well aware of God's contempt for the sin of pride. After relating the account of Nebuchadnezzar to Belshazzar, the prophet made a statement that I believe is the most chilling and sobering verse in the Old Testament:

"*And thou his son, 0 Belshazzar, hast not humbled thine heart, though thou knewest all this " (5:22).*

As awful as the sin of pride is in the mind of God, there is another sin that is even worse! I call this sin "the sin against light." Many vile acts are done under veil of darkness; some are blatantly committed in the cold light of day. Some are done without the sinner being fully aware of the fact of its wickedness; others are done in spite of the knowledge of God's view of it. This latter state is the worse.

Men hire killers to end the lives of men they hate. Women sell their bodies to the highest bidder. Dope peddlers ply their immoral trade by hooking school children on drugs. All of these are obviously beyond the range of the decent and the ethical. But in church services throughout the world there will be people present who are the very epitome of community goodness and personal piety, yet remain unsaved; and that sin is a sin against light and is considered more wicked by God than any other transgression committed by the most ungodly of men.

I mentioned the pride and homosexual abomination of Sodom and Gomorrah earlier. They never had the privilege of hearing Christ's gospel. Listen to the words of Jesus to the morally upright city of Capemaum as He takes them to task for their sin against the light that had been granted them:

"And thou. Capernaum, which art exalted unto heaven, shalt be brought down to hell: for if the mighty works, which have been done in thee, had been done in Sodom. it would have remained until this day. But I say unto you, that it shall be more tolerable in the day Q/'judgment. Than for thee "(Matthew 11:23-24).

Belshazzar had grown up as a boy in the court of Nebuchadnezzar. He had been a first-hand witness of his grandfather's humbling at the hand of God. He could not plead that he was ignorant of Daniel's reminder of Nebuchadnezzar's pride. Yet, he hardened his heart. Even God Almighty is unable to penetrate the heart made hard by a man's own choosing.

Every lost man, regardless of his reputation for uprightness, should remember that a failure to accept the salvation of Jesus Christ when it is so freely offered him is to sin against light and to put himself in the position of being against the God of heaven. Daniel scolded the king for his willful desecration of the vessels of God:

"But thou hast lifted up thyself against the Lord of heaven; and they have brought the vessels of his house before thee. and thou, and thy lords, thy wives. and thy concubines have drunk wine in them: and thou hast praised the gods of

silver, and gold. Of brass, iron, wood, and stone, which see not. nor hear, nor know; and the God in whose hand thy breath is, and whose are all thy ways, hast thou not glorified " (5:23).

The fear that had so gripped Belshazzar tightened its icy fingers about his throat as he nervously listened to the prophet. He was unable to speak, mesmerized by the hard words he was hearing. The quietness in the banquet hall was so thick it was impenetrable. Daniel's words were rolling toward the king like fortified warships riding the high crests of fast moving waves. It seemed they would never end. Each phrase, each word, each syllable sounded like dull, thudding gongs of judgment heavily being tolled on the leadened bell of eternity. Moments dragged by as Daniel continued his rebuke of the king with no attempt to do what he had been called to do—interpret the handwriting on the wall:

"And this is the writing that was written, MENE, MENE. TEKEL, UPHARSIN. This is the interpretation of the thing: MENE: God hatlt numbered thy kingdom, and finished it. TEKEL: Thou art weighed in the balances, and art found wanting. PERES: Thy kingdom is divided, and given to the Medes and Persians" (5:25-28).

Belshazzar was totally unprepared for the interpretation that he heard. His kingdom had been numbered, he had been weighed and found wanting. and his kingdom was about to be divided. Each of these deserve our attention:

(1) MENE: *. . God hath numbered thv kingdom, and finished it. .* Babylon was a world empire, but it was not a power that was feared in heaven. God had set limitations as to how far the nation would be allowed to extend its authority. Nation after nation had fallen beneath the onslaught of Babylon's apparently invincible armies. God was stopping it I all. Babylon had reached its deadline. Its day of regal rule was ended.

(2) TEKEL: *. . thou are weighed in the balances, and art found wanting. . .* "The ancient scales are familiar to those of us in our modem world, if for no other reason than their use as decorative pieces. These scales were made with a vertical stem on the top on which was poised a horizontal bar. At the ends of the bar were little containers suspended. One container held a pre-measured weight. Whatever was to be weighed was placed in the other container. If that container and weight

were too heavy, its end would be the lower end. If they were too light, they would be the higher.

Belshazzar thought of himself as a heavyweight, but in God's eyes he was a lightweight. Many a man thinks of civic awards, honors, and wealth as measurements of clout. But the only weight that will suffice when a man is placed on the scales of God's holiness is the blood of the Lord Jesus Christ.

(3) PERES: "... *thy kingdom is divided, and given to the Medes and Persians* ..." The word, "peres," is the singular form of "pharsin." The "u" in "upharsin" is the conjunction "and." The phrase might be translated, "Mene, mene, tekel, and pharsin (peres)."

This was the worst of the worst to Belshazzar! His kingdom was about to be taken from him. In ancient times, that meant that Belshazzar as king would die. Not only would he die, but the names of his executioners were given so that he could contemplate his doom.

"Then commanded Belshazzar, and they clothed Daniel with scarlet, and put a chain of gold about his neck, and made a proclamation concerning him, that he should be the third ruler in the kingdom. In that night was Belshazzar the king of the Chaldeans slain. And Darius the Median took the kingdom, being about threescore and two years old" (5:29-31)

We can only suppose what happened alter Belshazzar rewarded Daniel. Very likely, the king called for an emergency meeting of his generals and military strategists. With his mission now completed, the prophet watched the king in a state of hysteria begin barking out orders to his most trusted advisers and courtiers.

Turning his back upon the king for the last time, Daniel walked through the buzzing crowd and outside into the cool, night air. As he moved through the darkness, he sensed that something was astir, but feeling no conviction to do or say more, he collapsed into his bed, little realizing that he would be awakened before the dawn by the screams of dying men.

Back at the banquet hall, questions were being raised that demanded an answer. Was Daniel speaking the truth? Was he purposely deceiving the king?

Was Babylon vulnerable to an attack from the Medes and the Persians? Should the army be alerted?

Before any of these queries could be answered, the doors were flung open! Pouring into the hall were hordes of heavily-armed soldiers. Swords were flying and spears were being thrust into the soft flesh of dancing girls, ripping them apart like bloody rag dolls. Blood mingled with wine pooled on the marble floor. The lords of Babylon tried in vain to resist and were hacked and chopped by war axes like sides of beef in a butcher shop. When all was done, even the king lay on the floor with his life's blood running from cuts and wounds ail over his body. Finally, dead bodies were dragged from a hall reeking with the smell of liquor and death.

What had happened? Cyrus the Great led his combined forces of Medes and Persians to Babylon. Noting that the dimensions of the wall made it too high to scale and too thick to collapse by battering, he developed an ingenious plan. Building a darn up the Euphrates River from the city, he then dug a new riverbed into which the river could be redirected. Closing the gates of the dam, the Euphrates under the wall dried up, and he sent his soldiers under the wall to accomplish their bloody task.

It was October 11, 539 B.C., and Belshazzar was dead.

Chapter Six

Daniel In The Den Of Lions

One of the best-loved of Bible stories for children is found in this sixth chapter of the Book of Daniel. Countless boys and girls have been challenged and inspired by this incident in the life of courageous Daniel. There is a problem with the general presentation of this account, however. Daniel is usually portrayed as a teenage lad, but he was actually an old man past ninety years of age.

The lesson remains the same for young and old alike, God never fails the person who trusts in Him. Is it not comforting to know that as the years come swiftly upon us, our Lord stands staunchly beside us to be a sure supporter and defender against every adversity?

An artist captured the essence of what actually happened in the lions' den. He depicted, in a very impressive manner, the reliance of Daniel upon the God of glory. The lions are seen standing and lying passively all about Daniel with their mouths closed. His eyes are not fixed in fear on the lions, nor are his eyes closed in prayer; rather, they are triumphantly looking upward towards heaven and God. The source of power back then, as it always has been and will be, is in God.

I am reminded of the corporate representative who was sent to India. Having a fear of snakes already, he was especially frightened of the deadly cobra. He feverishly undertook the task of learning everything that he could about the snake. Soon, he was well-versed in where the cobra might most likely be found, the most dangerous areas to avoid, etc. Upon his arrival in India, he was given a companion to serve as a guide and was simply instructed to follow the leadership of that guide and no harm would befall him. Did that include snakes? Yes, that included snakes. As long as he stayed near his guide and heeded his warnings, he would be in no danger whatever. Unfortunately, he could not force himself to simply trust his guide, and as a result, saw cobras where there weren't cobras. Finally, in nervous exhaustion, he returned in failure to the United States without ever once seeing one of the deadly cobra snakes.

His awful dilemma resulted from too much attention on the enemy and not enough attention on the one who was his protector. I certainly believe that we are prudent to measure the strength of the enemies and problems that confront us, but I also think that we are foolish indeed if we give inordinate amounts of concentration upon them instead of the Lord.

Take, for example, the matter of demons. Without question, demonology is a valid Biblical doctrine and they are definitely active in the world today; in fact, they may be even more prevalent in their deceptive influence than during the time of Christ on earth. Knowing that the believer's victory is accomplished by the saint looking to the cross, Satan will do anything, including the detailed study of the devil himself, to remove the Christian's eyes from Calvary. How subtle this sinister enemy of the saint can be!

The den of lions is an experience in the life of Daniel that reveals the fundamental bedrock foundation upon which he had built his life. He always looked to God! Every other challenge in this book was met in the same confident manner as the one with the lions—he expectantly kept his eyes on God!

Simon Peter learned that lesson well. As he boldly walked through the waves toward Jesus, he had no difficulty at all until he took his eyes off the Lord. The very moment he moved his eyes from the face of Christ, and furtively looked at the lightning, the billowing black clouds, and the thrashing waves, Peter began to sink. The very water that had threatened to destroy Peter and the other disciples was already under the Master's feet; as long as Peter faced Christ, they were under his feet, too. Dear Reader, all your pressing problems that threaten you are under the feet of Jesus. As long as you completely trust Him, they will be under your feet, too. As the hymn writer has well said:

Turn your eyes upon Jesus, book full in His wonderful face, And the things of earth will grow strangely dim, In the light of His glory and grace.

Remember, Daniel was an old man. Yet, he was still in the service of God. Often we hear older churchmembers, who have been faithful in positions of leadership for many years, talk about stepping down and letting younger people assume the tasks that they have been performing. But that is not found among the nobler saints in the Word of God. They worked hard for the Lord until they died or God took them home to be with Him! As one old preacher told me many years ago, "If I must be a pile of something at the end of my life, I would rather be a pile of ashes than a pile of dust. I would rather burn out as rust out."

Some of the world's great men made their best and most productive contributions in their latter years. Gladstone became prime minister of England at the age of 83. Michelangelo painted his masterpiece, "The Final Judgement," on the ceiling of the Sistine Chapel in Vatican City at the age of 89. J. C. Penney was still working daily in his corporate offices at the age of 95. John Wesley preached some of his most powerful and brilliant sermons at the age of 88. The inimitable preacher, R. G. Lee, was still crisscrossing America and preaching with amazing skill at the age of 89. Age is no excuse in the service of God.

Daniel 6: 1-2 introduces to us a man by the name of Darius the Median, who, according to the previous chapter, took the throne for the Medo-Persians after the victory over Belshazzar. Darius was a common Persian name, so we cannot be sure about the identity of him. He might have been Cambyses who was the son of Cyrus. He could have been one of the higher-ranking Persian rulers, Gubaru. Or, it is possible that this was a name for Cyrus. Whomever he was, one thing is certain. He was a good administrator in government.

Please note his wisdom in dividing the responsibilities of the kingdom in verses one and two:

"It pleased Darius to set over the kingdom an hundred and twenty princes, which should be over the whole kingdom; and over these three presidents; of whom Daniel was first: that the princes might give accounts unto them, and the king should have no damage."

Darius the Median knew that the best chance for the survival of government was in the division of power, the multiplicity of rulers. Obviously, he was primarily concerned with ability to lead, rather than relationship to the one in power. Recognizing special gifts of Daniel, Darius immediately placed this who had been in exile with his nation under Belshazzar Babylon, into a position of exalted leadership:

"Then this Daniel was preferred above the presidents and princes, because an excellent spirit was in him; and the king thought to set him aver the

whole realm" (Daniel 6:3).

Why was Daniel preferred by Darius? He was preferred because "an excellent spirit was in him. " This spirit was the result of his walking with God and trusting Him through all the experiences of his life. But even more, Daniel was a man whose prayer life was the top priority in his daily routine, as we shall see later in our study of this chapter. His time with God was highly valued by him!

But I think in addition to these noble spiritual qualities, Daniel was a humble man who refused to allow himself to be trapped by the snare of an envious attitude toward others who might be enjoying greater success than he at a given time. The Bible tells us that envy is *"rottenness of the bone. "* You can find no evidence whatever that Daniel was at any time in his life a jealous and vindictive person.

The extraordinary thing about it all is that Daniel had been forcefully removed from his homeland. He had been witness to the horrible spectacle of the temple being desecrated and destroyed by the invading Babylonian hordes. He had been subjected to recurring life-threatening challenges from those in authority over him. For these reasons, and perhaps many others that we will never know, Daniel would have from the human standpoint been justified in having bitter attitudes toward his captors, be they Babylonian or be they Persian. It is an overlooked miracle that he was not.

However, he was the recipient of malicious envy from those over whom he was placed. Why? Well, Daniel had been successful. Success is sweet but it also brings moments made sour by the cruel barbs and tacky remarks of those in the same peer group who are losers.

Nobody ever criticizes a loser. On one occasion in my early ministry, I went through a period of depression. Stretched out on the living room floor in our parsonage one afternoon, I reached out my hand to a tape recorder on which I had earlier been listening to a taped sermon by the great preacher, Dr. B. R. Lakin. An angel surely must have arranged for his sermon to be at exactly the right spot when I switched the recorder on. The first thing I heard was Dr. Lakin saying in his quaint, old-fashioned way, "If you ever start getting kicked in the behind, just keep moving forward, because it means you are out front." Success brings criticism!

It would have been much better for these detractors of Daniel had they chosen to join him rather than oppose. I have observed that if you associate with winners, you become a winner; if you associate with losers, you become a loser. If there was ever a winner, it was Daniel! But they chose to find some fault with which to accuse him before the king:

"Then the presidents and princes sought to find occasion against Daniel concerning the kingdom: but they could find none occasion nor fault: forasmuch as he was faithful, neither was there any error or fault in him. Then said these men, we shall not find any occasion against this Daniel. except we find it against him concerning the law of his God" (Daniel 6:4-5).

Here is a characteristic of Daniel that should be the trademark of every believer. He *". . . Was faithful, neither was there any error or fault found in him. "* Daniel was as obedient to the governmental authorities of the Persians as he had been previously to those of Babylon. God's people are to be good, law-abiding citizens. They are never to be proponents of civil disobedience which is an anti-scriptural philosophy that exhorts its adherents to refuse compliance with any law that displeases him. That is not the teaching of God's Word. Listen to words of Paul in Romans 13:1-4:

"Let every soul be subject unto the higher powers. For there is no power but of God: the powers that be are ordained of God. Whasoever there/'ore resisteth the power. resisteth the ordinance of God: and they that resist shall receive to themselves damnation. For rulers are not a terror to good works, but to the evil. Wilt thou then not be ti/Faid of the power? Do that which is good, and thou shalt have praise of the same. For he is the minister of God to thee for good. But if thou do that which is evil, be afraid,-for he beareth not the sword in vain: for he is the minister of God, a revenger to execute wrath upon him that doeth evil. "

Daniel recognized and willingly obeyed the law of the state in all instances—except one. He never failed to abide by governmental regulations unless they were in direct conflict with the commands of God. This identical commitment was made by Peter in Acts 5:29:

"Then Peter and the other apostles answered and said, We ought to obey God rather than men. "

Watch the subtle deviousness of the enemies of Daniel as their plan to destroy him unfolds. They knew that the only way to bring Daniel under the wrath of the crown was to set up a situation in which his religious "convictions would be in opposition to the directives of the king. Only then would Daniel defy the royal orders and appear to be a traitor, disloyal to the will of Darius.

These vindictive men had construed an unbeatable plan. Daniel was a man who would not deny the Lord regardless of the personal consequences; Darius, the king, was a man who placed tremendous importance on keeping one's word. This characteristic of absolute integrity was a trademark of ancient Persian rulers as we will discuss in detail in chapter eleven of our study. But for now, note particularly in verse eight that Darius was reminded of that custom as these cruel men presented their plan to the king:

"Then these presidents and princes assembled together to the king, and said thus unto him, King Darius. live forever. All the presidents, of the kingdom. The governors, and the princes. The counselors, and the captains, have consulted together to establish a royal statute, and to make a firm decree. That whosoever shall ask a petition of any God or man for thirty days, save of thee, 0 king, he shall be cast into the den of lions. Now, 0 king, establish the decree, and sign the writing, that it be not changed, according to the law of the Medes and Persians, which altereth not" (Daniel 6:8-9)

Did you notice that the king's decree prohibited anyone in the kingdom from praying for thirty days? To be sadly honest, it would matter very little to the modem churchmember if such a regulation from our government were passed today. Most people simply do not pray. It is not a burning daily desire to them. But Daniel was a man who thrived on prayer. He was deeply in love with God. He looked forward to those times each day that afforded him a special intimacy with the Father. Verse 10 tells us several things about his devotional prayer times that ought to be true for every believer:

"Now when Daniel knew that the writing was signed. he went into his

house; and his windows being open in his chamber Toward Jerusalem, he kneeled upon his knees three times a day, and prayed, and gave thanks before his God, as he did aforetime" (6:10).

Let us examine, by dissecting this verse, the traits of Daniel's prayer life. His prayer was marked by its:

(1) PLACE: "*. . . he went into his house; and his windows being opened in his chamber toward Jerusalem . . .*" Oh, how thankful I am that Daniel did not grumble or complain. He just turned on his heel after hearing the news of the king's decree and went straight to meet God in prayer.

His place of prayer was his home with the windows open. He did not alter his prayers in order to conceal that he was praying. Obviously, there was a definite area within the house that had been dedicated by Daniel as his prayer altar.

Dick Eastman, speaker for Change The World School of Prayer, says that every believer should have a "gap," his word for the prayer closet. Your gap may be your bedroom, your basement, your kitchen table, or even your bathroom. You a place, a definite place, to which you will almost be drawn when problems come.

Dear Reader, do you have a place of prayer? Find your spot. Use your imagination. As you daily resort to that for your personal time of communion with God, you will find a brand new sweetness and vitality for your Christian walk. The difficult situations of life will become springboards from which your prayer will catapult you into new realms of faith victories.

(2) POSTURE: *. . he kneeled upon his knees. . .* " I do Not subscribe to any particular position as being the only position from which a person can effectively seek the Lord, but I enjoy getting down on my knees or even lying full-length on the floor.

There just seems to be an atmosphere, an attitude, of humility when I lower myself to my knees. Of course, from the most ancient of days, men knelt before the one to whom they were in allegiance. It was a gesture of respect and required protocol for a person entering a throne room to sink to his knees immediately upon his entrance through the door.

How much more should we reverence the King of kings and Lord of lords! The sincere believer should come to his V designated place of prayer and emotionally, if not indeed physically, kneel before God before making the requests that brought him to the Father.

That posture is best achieved by beginning the prayer time with meditation of who God is and of what He has done. We ought to avoid treating God with the flippancy and casual attitude we ordinarily exhibit toward waitresses. bank tellers. and short order cooks. He is the omnipotent God and Creator of all that exists. How can we so foolishly presume that we have the audacious gall to strut into His wondrous presence as though we are doing Him a favor by coming'? He is God. High and lifted up!

(3) PREVALENCE: . . *three times a day*. . ."Daniel did not skip a day or spend one time in the morning or evening with God. Instead, he got alone with God three times each day.

Someone may object by saying that there just is not enough time because of daily routines being so busy. How often we complain that there is not enough time in the day to do all that we are required!

That is actually an indictment of ourselves! God never gives a person so much to do that he does not have sufficient time to do it well and with grace. The frenzied, mile-a-minute Christian who is being pulled in forty different directions is no   compliment to the guidance and providence of God.

We have so crammed our waking hours with good things that the best things are left undone or relegated to less than the position of highest priority. Day after day we continue to attempt many good things, but few best things.

This is even true in the realm of the religious. People often "meet themselves" going back and forth to church activities, giving little thought to the possibility that Christ may not even be pleased with it all. Hence, what we do we measure in terms of quantity, while what we do he measures in quality. That means that much of our work equals nothing more than "wood, hay, and stubble," that will be fit for nothing in light of eternal values and will, therefore, be burned in the fires of judgement.

It probably goes without saying that a daily routine that includes multiple periods of prayer can go a long way toward getting all of life's other activities into proper focus. Knowing what pleases God is far more worthwhile than attempting to please others-even the ego of oneself.

(4) PURPOSE: *. . gave thanks before his God. . ."* Daniel recognized the importance of praise and thanksgiving. He may not have been thanking God for the problem that had come his way; sometimes that is easier said than done, but he was expressing his deep gratitude to God. Even if we cannot see any way that good can come from the dark dilemmas in which we may sometimes find ourselves, is comforting to know that God will turn the ashes of into blossoms of blessings, even if He must do it in that require the passage of great lengths of time. We can God that He is God!

Verse 11 tells us that Daniel also made supplication. The meaning of supplication is more than praying. It is to reason with God, to figure out with our Lord what He is doing in and through the personal traumas that are plaguing you. If we could only fully comprehend the scope of how much our loving Heavenly Father wants to do on our behalf. If you need help in making your petitions known to Him, you might use this little acrostic on the word ACTS.

"A" is for "ADORATION." Start your time of prayer by adoring God, particularly His son, Jesus. Jesus is God's "only begotten Son. "If you want the favor of a mother, brag on her child. So it is with God. It pleases the Father to hear your words of praise heaped on Jesus.

"C" is for "CONFESSION." The psalmist reports in Psalm 66:18: "If I regard iniquity in my heart, the Lord will not hear me. " Unconfessed sin ruptures the clear channel from man to God. Confession is vital:

"If we confess our sins, he is faithful and just to forgive us our sins, and to cleanse us from all unrighteousness"(I John 1:9).

"T" is for "THANKSGIVING." We must follow the example of Daniel and send upward to God the gratitude of our hearts. I am thoroughly convinced that ingratitude is the gravest of all sins.

"S" is for "SUPPLICATION." After we have adored the Son, confessed our sins, and thanked God for all that He has done, we are then ready to ask for the meeting of our needs. Try this little formula and I believe it will be a blessing.

(5) PERSISTENT: *. . as he did aforetime. . .*" Some people must be driven to their knees. The only times that prayer becomes needful for them is when emergencies arise. God wants us to love Him for who He is! He wants us to long for Him just to be near Him! His desire is that we want Him, not what He can do for us. Continual prayer, in good times and bad, honors Him.

Daniel prayed! Where were his critics? The Bible does not tell us, but it is evident that they knew where he was and what he was doing. They found him praying, in violation of the king's royal command:

"Then these men assembled, and found Daniel praying and making supplication before his God" (Daniel 6:11).

How hard would someone have to look to find you in prayer? Would your critics even know where you pray?

How jubilant these haters of Daniel must have been as they bounded back to the palace like hounds of hell, deliciously licking their lips with the satisfaction of the successful accomplishment of their evil deed. Everything was moving precisely to plan. Now, all that was lacking was the final sentencing of Daniel by the king. And, as already mentioned earlier, they were well aware of the high value that the Persians placed on honesty and the keeping of pledges.

Darius was a noble man with a heart of great love for these people, like Daniel, who had shown themselves as being loyal and honorable. When he realized the severity of the problem that it had resulted, in part, from his own hand, Darius was grieved. Listen for the moaning of his heart in these verses:

"Then the king, when he heard these words, was sore displeased with himself and set his heart on Daniel to deliver him: and he labored till the going down of the sun to deliver him . . . then the king went to his palace, and passed the

night fasting: neither were instruments of music brought before him: and his sleep went from him . . . and when he came to the den, he cried with s lamentable voice unto Daniel " (6:14, 18, 20).

What a night of misery the king spent! His faithful supporter, was in the den of lions because of his carelessness in to the advice of wicked men. Just before throwing to the lions, however, the king made a statement of prophecy without even realizing it:

"Then the king commanded, and they brought Daniel, and cast him into the den of lions. Now the king spake and said unto Daniel, thy God whom thou serves! continually, he will deliver thee" (6:17).

Even pagans, when the "chips are down," are forced to admit that the God of heaven is equal to all challenges. But ironically, most lost people are just like Darius. What he accepted as fact he did not put into practice. He knew that the God of Israel, Jehovah, was indeed Lord over every calamity. It is strange that men come to such conclusions, only to fall short of embracing the lovely Lord. The old preachers spoke of such experiences as "having your hand on the very doorknob of
heaven but sliding backward into hell."

Unlike the king, Daniel spent a peaceful night in the lions' den. It is far better to be in the throes of apparently overwhelming difficulty if it is God's will for you to be there than it is to be out of God's will in a place that the world says is safe.

What happened? The Bible triumphantly proclaims that God sent an angel. Even a great number of savage lions are no match for an angel. In another Biblical account, one angel in one night killed 185 .000 well-trained soldiers in Sennacherib's army when they had surrounded Jerusalem, when Hezekiah was king. Please note the victory in Daniel's response to the king's call to him:

"My God hath sent his angel, and hath shut the lions ' mouth, that they have not hurt me, forasmuch as before him innocence was found in me; and also before thee, 0 king, have I done no hurt" (6:22).

I imagine that the scene in heaven may have gone something like this. God heard Daniel's prayer from his room. Intently watching the unfolding events on earth, God turns to one of His angels and says, "*Go down there and take care of Daniel, I don't have many righteous men so want him kept alive. Don't you let a single one of those overgrown pussycats even scare him with a half snarl. So, get on down there.*"

That angel, in a flash, headed toward earth. Arriving just ahead of Daniel in the lions' den, he called a quick meeting of the lions club. I can hear him saying, "*Listen now! Your creator has sent me down here to tell you guys that the king is about to throw a man down here. And God doesn't want him bothered--at all! Besides, he's a tough old customer who's been through enough already. I've been sent here to make sure that you leave him alone. If you lay one paw on him, I'll make catnip tea out of you!*"

When Daniel came tumbling down into the den, all he found were some yawning lions lazily moving around, with their tawny tails gently swaying. He may have even used one of the beasts for a pillow.

A very interesting phrase is found in verse 22: ". . . *Also before thee, O king, have I done no hurt.* " In other words, Daniel was assuring the king that he was uninjured. But almost humorously, he wanted the king to know that he had not hurt the lions, nor the king, either. In other words. I believe the real meaning here is not physical injury. That would be absurd since the king was surely surrounded by several bodyguards. I prefer to believe that Daniel, being the loyal person that he was, did nothing to embarrass the king's position, even if it meant at the risk of his own life.

Oh, how happy the king was upon hearing the good news that Daniel was alive. Verse 23 proclaims:

"Then was the king exceeding glad for him, and commanded that they should take Daniel up out of the den. and no 'manner of hurt was found upon him, because he believed m his God.

Now, let me ask you a question. How many men were cast into the lions' den? The answer is one. How many spent the night in the lions' den? That answer is two. How many came out of the den? This final answer is one. Daniel was thrown into the den, an angel met him there, but Daniel came out of the den by himself

This is a marvelous truth in this bit of Biblical fact. God wants to bear our burdens for us. Daniel left his problem of the lions with the Lord!

Dear Reader, cast your cares upon Jesus. Why should you insist on shouldering the difficulty of life alone when Jesus does not want you to carry even part of it? I believe that there are two common errors made by most of us. We assume responsibilities that really are God's; or, we want God to assume responsibilities that really belong to us. If you can only learn to practice the principle of releasing your cares to Him, you will be immeasurably blessed.

It must be remembered that God did not destroy the lions. Sometimes we desire of God that He will cause our adversities to evaporate, to disappear. The lions were still there. Verse 22 says that God . . *hath shut the lions' mouths*. . ." Although Daniel was in the very presence of his animal enemies for an extended period of time, they were rendered totally incapable of harming him.

He could have lived those hours in constant fear that at any moment they would attack him, but he did not. We must learn that God does not always choose to rid us of our problems, but he will keep-them from destroying us. Remember God's promise in Isaiah 54:17:

"No weapon that is formed against thee shall prosper, and every tongue that shall rise against thee in judgment thou shalt condemn. This is the heritage of the servants of the Lord, and their righteousness is from me, saith the Lord. "

God kept this promise. Not only did He provide security for Daniel, but those who schemed against the prophet were themselves, along with their families, cast into the den of lions. God takes care of His own!

Chapter Seven

Prophecies of World Empires

Our Heavenly Father cares so very much for His children that He chose to provide clearly detailed information about coming days. The most easily distinguishable feature that separates the Bible from all of the world's other religious books is that the Word of God makes exact prophetic statements that must be precisely fulfilled or recognized as completely in error. This chapter is the opening chapter of the second half of the book. Even as the first six chapters are primarily concerned with Daniel's personal life, the final seven chapters are, in the main, developed around some truly remarkable prophecies. These divine predictions encourage the beleaguered believer in his walk through the maze of a confused and confusing religious world by showing him through the proof of fulfilled prophecies that God is faithful.

In the Old Testament can be found sheer multitudes of prophetic statements that cover a host of various subjects. Virtually every aspect of the life of Christ as well as the huge number of intricate details surrounding His second coming in glory are all the subjects of the Old Testament writers' concern. Fundamentally, these prophetic statements in the Old Testament serve three functions:

(l) They gloriously depict the appearing of Christ as messiah;

(2) They confirm God's faithfulness in the keeping of His promises. In so doing, the Bible student is assured that if God kept a part of His Word, we can trust Him to keep the rest of it. For example, when we see that Jesus was indeed born in Bethelehem Ephratah, just as Micah had foretold so many years earlier, and had foretold in such unmistakable detail, we have firm support for the confidence that future prophecies will just as surely be performed.

(3) They authenticate the Bible as God's Word because the detailed fulfillment of prophecies occurring after hundreds of years have passed from the time of the utterance of the prophetic statement can only be explained as being done by the hand of God. Isaiah expressed the identical conviction:

DANIEL

"Remember this, and shew yourselves men: bring it again to mind. O ye transgres.r0rs,- remember the former things of old, for I am God, and there is none else; I am God. and there is none like me; declaring the end from the beginning, and from ancient times the things that are not yet done. saying, my counsel shall stand, and I will do all my pleasure" (Isaiah 46:9-10).

God is omniscient! He knows all! And God's plan for the ages is well articulated in His Word. That is the very reason that I assert that the Bible is:

Infallible -- There are no flaws;

Inerrant -- It is absolutely without error;

Verbally-Inspired - Each word is inspired, not just the thoughts;

Plenary —— All of the Bible is equally inspired of God.

But we must always remember. Regardless of the authority of its words or the majesty of its expressions, the Bible is not the object of our worship: It is the singularly reliable signpost toward eternity, but we must always remember that it is Christ who will take us home. The end of our search for God is not on the Bible's printed page but rather through the page to the face of its author, our Lord Jesus Christ. The Bible is not so much the way to God as He is the way to the Bible. Salvation is not in the Book; salvation is in the Book's Author.

Chapter seven, verse one, introduces us again to Belshazzar, king of Babylon. But, as we have already seen, Belshazzar was slain by the invasion of the city by the Medes and the Persians in Daniel 5:30. Chapter seven, therefore, is not in chronological as it follows chapter six. It is a recounting of an incident in the life of Daniel that occurred in the first year of Belshazzar's reign but paralleled the dream of Nebuchadnezzar about the metallic man in chapter two.

Verse two describes the four winds of heaven as they blow '. . . *the great sea.* " Of course, this sea might be a reference to the Mediterranean Sea, but I believe that it is not. i.e. the balance of the vision is heavily symbolic, it is only that this "sea" is, too. This symbol is used in identifying at rolling masses of the ungodly Gentile masses. Isaiah his way:

"Then thou shalt see, and flow together, and thine heart shall fear. and be enlarged, because the abundance of the sea shall be converted unto thee, the forces of the Gentiles shall come thee" (60:5).

Before we launch into our examination of Daniel's dream, it is imperative that you recognize that the dream of Nebuchadnezzar in chapter two and the dream of Daniel in chapter seven are both discussions of the same prophecy. Nebuchadnezzar's metallic man had a head of gold (representing the Babylonian), arms of silver (representing the Medo-Persian Empire), Abdomen in of brass (representing the Grecian Empire). Daniel's dream is of an eagle (representing the Babylonian Empire), a Bear (representing the Medo-Persian Empire), a leopard (representing the Grecian Empire), and a beast with iron teeth (representing the Roman Empire).

Why are there two visions necessary to identify the empires that would rule in the world? Very simply, the metallic Man is the world's view of itself. The world sees its social order as shining and beautiful. It is a world of strength, of almost unlimited power in its own capacities. God, however, does not look upon this world order as a work of art. He sees it as a
vastly jungle, wild and untamed.

How do you see yourself, as a self-made work of art or a man who, unless saved and a new creature in Christ, is capable of the most hideous of sins? Jeremiah 17:9 says:

"The heart is deceitful above all things, and desperately wicked: who can know it?"

There is nothing of beauty within the unregenerated man to recommend him to God and merit salvation for him:

"For I know that in me (that is, in my flesh,) dwelleth no good thing: for to will is present with me; but how to perjbrm that which is good I find not" (Romans 7:18).

Egotistical man will not humble himself before the righteousness of God.

He cannot within himself believe that his ethics and deeds of humanity are considered by the Lord as nothing more than filthy rags. Man sees himself as a glittering metallic man; God sees him as a beast! Unless an individual comes to the place of accepting his own worthlessness, he will never be saved. Individuals, churches, families, or nations that have the "metallic man" image of themselves are doomed.

Beginning in Daniel 7:4, let us take a look at each of the symbolic animals:

"The first was like a lion, and had eagle's wings; I beheld till its wings thereof were plucked, and it was lifted up from the earth, and made stand upon the feet as a man; and a man's heart was given to it."

Archaeologists have uncovered ancient emblems of the Babylonians. One very prominent insignia was that of a lion with eagle's wings. The parallel vision of Nebuchadnezzar in chapter two, verses 37 and 38, describes Babylon in this manner:

"Thou, O king, art a king of kings; for the God of heaven hath given thee a kingdom, power, and strength, and glory. And wherever the children of men dwell, the beasts of the field and the fowls of the heavens hath he given into thine hand, and hath made thee ruler over them all. Thou art this head of gold."

What is the meaning of the phrase "... *its wings were plucked*..."? (7:4). As grand as the empire of the Babylonians may have been, it was still subject to the power of God. The limitations of man's endeavors have been established by the Lord, and He knows exactly how to contain ambitious individuals or nations within the boundaries of their pre-determined spheres. Another phrase, ..*a man's heart was to it* ..."is a reference to the experience of humbling that crushed the proud heart of Babylon's most famous leader, Nebuchadnezzar.

The lion is known for his prowess, but the second symbolic animal in Daniel's vision is the bear, known for its strength:

"And, behold. another beast, a second, like a bear. and it raised up itself

on one side, and it had three ribs in the mouth of it between its teeth; and they said thus unto it, arise, devour much flesh" (7:5).

This bear pictures the combined forces of the Medes and the Persians. Neither of these nations had a chance in an invasion against mighty Babylon. In fact, even in combination, they were decided underdogs. In Nebuchadnezzar's dream, this inferiority is literally stated:

"*And after thee shall arise another kingdom inferior to thee . . .*" (Daniel 2:39).

The "*three ribs*" mentioned in verse five is a probable allusion to the new empire of Media, Persia, and Babylon. Verse five exhorts this new empire to ". . . *arise, devour much flesh.* " Along with the remaining outlying areas of Babylon, two other nations were beginning to flex their imperialistic muscles. These two were Lydia and Egypt. Ultimately, these countries also met the same fate as Babylon as they fell beneath the crush of the advancing Medo-Persian armies.

Verse six presents the third animal, one that is known by its speed, the leopard. The Medo-Persian Empire with all of its brute strength, fell to the swiftness of the Greeks under the leadership of Alexander the Great. It was Alexander who followed in the steps of Philip of Macedon in developing innovative warfare. His Grecian troops were virtually un- stoppable as he introduced swift horses and weapon-equipped chariots to the battlefield. Alexander's military strategies were so ahead of his time, and his armies moved so rapidly, there was no nation that could stop him from the achieving of his desired goals. In fact, in the decisive battle with the Persians which would determine his world domination, he sent only 60,000 men against an enemy army of over one million men. Yet, the enemy was utterly vanquished. The "*wings of a fowl*" is a phrase that adds even more credence to the rapid movement of his troops.

Verse six also shares another interesting detail of prophecy that happened just as Daniel had said. Note the phrase, . . *The beast had four heads*." Historically, Alexander the Great had four generals as powers in his hierarchy of leadership who exerted more control than any others in his military/political staff of advisors. These four were:
(1) Cassander;

Lysimachus;
Ptolemy I;
(4) Seleucus.

This same prophecy of the Grecian domination over the world was also witnessed by Nebuchadnezzar in his dream:

. . and another third kingdom of brass, which shall bear rule over all the earth" (2:39).

Onward we move in Daniel's dream to chapter seven, verse seven for a view of the final of the four beasts:

'After this I saw in the night visions, and, behold, a fourth beast. dreadful and terrible, and strong exceedingly, and it had great iron teeth; it devoured and broke in pieces, and stamped the residue with its feet; and it was diverse from all the beasts that were before it, and it had ten horns " (7:7).

This verse is somewhat of a summary verse in prophecy. It spans the years separating the old Roman Empire all way to the end of the age with the re-establishment of the influence under the antichrist. Note also that the entire age is skipped in the verse. You will also notice that the empires were defeated by the nations succeeding but no nation was prophesied by Daniel as the conqueror Rome. And guess what! The Roman Empire was not the of another nation's ambitious designs, they destroyed from within.

Nebuchadnezzar's dream also included the Roman Empire:

"And the fourth kingdom shall be strong as iron, forasmuch as iron breaketh in pieces and subdueth all things; and, as iron that breaketh all these, shall it break in pieces and bruise. And whereas thou sawest the feet and toes, part of potters clay and part iron, the kingdom shall be divided; but there shall be in it of the strength of the iron, forasmuch as thou sawest the iron mixed with miry clay. And as the toes of the feet were part of iron and part of clay, so the kingdom shall be partly strong and partly broken. And whereas thou sawest iron mixed with miry clay, they shall mingle themselves with the seed of men; but they shall not cleave one to another, even as iron is not mixed with clay" (Daniel 2:40-43).

But we do have some striking contrasts between the dream in chapter two and the dream of Daniel in seven. Both of these have references to something that ten in symbolism, but the symbols for those ten things different. In Daniel 7:7 we have ten horns; in Daniel 2:24 have ten toes. To rightly interpret the meanings of these symbols, let us turn to Revelation 13:

"and I stood upon the sand of the sea, and saw a beast rise up out of the sea having seven heads and ten horns. . ." (13: 1).

This is the great "antichrist chapter" in the Bible. Remember that we have already shown that "sea," when symbolically used, is a reference to the Gentile nations. This beast rising up out of the sea is antichrist, the last great world ruler, and among other identifying marks, he has ten horns. To determine the things being symbolized by these horns, we must move to Revelation 17:12:

"And the ten horns which thou sawest are ten kings, who have received no kingdom as yet, but receive power as kings one hour with the beast. "

This verse conforms exactly with Daniel 7:24 which says:

"And the ten horns out of this kingdom are ten kings that shall arise. . ."

By combining these verses, we now have a clear definitive understanding of the symbols. The toes in Daniel 2 and the horns in Daniel 7 both refer to a ten-nation confederacy that will be led by the antichrist at the end of time. I believe that the fulfillment of this prophecy may very well be in the modem European Economic Community (EEC), better known as the Common Market, which was founded under the authorization of the Treaty of Rome in 1954.

Unquestionably, the "*little horn* " of Daniel 7:8 is a reference to some little king or kingdom. Obviously, since this little horn gains control of the other horns, it is a reference to the antichrist of the thirteenth chapter of Revelation: The phrase, ". . . a mouth speaking great thing, " in Daniel 7:8, parallels perfectly with a statement made of the antichrist in Revelation 13:5:

"And there was given unto him a mouth speaking great things and blasphemies, and power was given unto him to continue forty and two months."

Returning to the seventh chapter of Daniel, we realize that our view of the coming empires of the world has ended. Verse nine gives us a spectacular view of the throne of God upon which is seated ". . . *The Ancient of days.* "This title for our Lord is repeated again in verse 13 and again in verse 22. The atmosphere conveyed in verses 9 and 10 is that of the judgment.

Although there are many who erroneously teach a general before which both the saved and the lost must stand, it here to say that the Bible in no place teaches such a On the contrary, there is a judgment for the lost "*the great white throne judgment*"; there is a judgment the saved called "*the judgment seat of Christ.* " It should be noted that neither of the two judgments will determine salvation: that determination will have already been made by individual during his lifetime on earth. In fact, the judgment sins was borne for every man by Jesus Christ at Calvary. no place in the Scriptures teach that a man will be or his sins; he is judged for his works. For the saved, the is solely for the accurate bestowal of rewards upon For the unsaved at his judgment, the only question to be is his degree of punishment.

Consider the following verses on the judgment:

"He that believeth on him is not condemned (judged); but he that believeth not is condemned (iudged) already, because he hath not believed in the name of the only begotten Son of God " (John 3:18).

A stronger and more emphatic statement about the saved not appearing before God for the judgment of his sins to determine whether he will finally be saved or lost is found in John 5:24:

"Verily, verily, I say unto you, he that heareth my word, and believeth on him that sent rne, hath everlasting Ii/2. ', and shall not come into condemnation (judgment), but is passed from death unto life. "

Oh, praise His dear name that we do not live in awful anticipation of a judgment day where the sins we have committed could result in our being cast into hell. As the hymn ' writer said:

> *"Jesus paid it all, All to Him I owe, Sin had left a crimson stain, He washed it white as snow. "*

Scriptures abound that assure us of the victory we have in Jesus:

> *"There is therefore now no condemnation to them who are in Christ Jesus, who walk not after the flesh, but after the Spirit"(Romans 8:1).*

However, the believer's works must be judged. In II Corinthians 5:10 is a solemn warning to every Christian who might be tempted to take his appearance before our Lord too lightly:

> *"For we must all appear before the judgment seat of Christ, that everyone may receive the things done in his body, according to that he hath done, whether it be good or bad. "*

Having established that all men, both saved and lost, must appear before God, exactly which person of the Godhead will be the judge? Will it be the Father, the Son, or the Holy Ghost? In other words, who is Daniel's *"Ancient of Days"*? The Bible leaves no doubt! turn to John 5:22:

> *"For the Father judgeth no man; but hath committed all judgment unto the Son. "*

Now, moving to Acts 17:31, let us listen to the words of Paul on this important subject:

> *"Because he hath appointed a day, in which he will judge the world in righteousness by that man whom he hath ordained; concerning which he hath given assurance unto all men, in that he hath raised him from the dead. "*

It is upon these verses that the agnostic will mount his venomous attack!

How can Christ be the judge? How can the Son of Mary born in Bethlehem's manger be the Ancient of Days? There is no problem nor contradiction for the faithful Bible student who accepts as fact the triune personality of God. Jesus was God placed in human flesh at Bethlehem, but Jesus was also in existence as God before the world began. In the first chapter of John's gospel are these memorable words:

"In the beginning was the Word, and the Word was with God, and the Word was God. The same was in the beginning with God. All things were made by him; and without him was not anything made that was made . . . and the Word was made flesh, and dwelt among us (and we beheld his glory, the glory as of the only begotten of the Father), full of grace and truth "
(John 1:1-3; 14).

Since we are discussing this matter of the judgment, let us consider what the Bible says will be the manner by which we are judged. In other words, although it has not been generally recognized, there will be a rather definite difference in the attitude of God toward those who stand before Him. Matthew 7:1-2 says:

':Judge not, that ye be not judged. For with what judgment ye Judge, ye shall be judged; and with what measure ye mete, it shall be measured to you again."

Make no mistake! The way that you look at others will be the way that God will look at you! A very practical Biblical principle of the coming day of judgment is shared in these verses. If you look with criticism at the life of your brother, overlooking his finer qualities so that you may dwell on his weaknesses and faults, God will in like manner overlook your finer qualities to dwell on your weaknesses and faults. However, if you look with compassion past the obvious frailties of your brother, God will look with compassion past your frailties to the more nobler traits in your life. Oh, may God grant us the discipline and self-control to choose the latter rather than the

Returning again to Daniel 7-9, please note the garment of the Ancient of Days (Christ) is white, a symbol of His purity and sinlessness, and His hair is like pure wool, another reference to His sinless character that gives Him the exclusive right to judge sinful men. Fire is twice mentioned in the same verse, and fire is always a Biblical reference to God's all-seeing, all-knowing, discernment in the affairs of men. The wheels of this throne is a reference to the always moving never- ending aspect of His judgment.

As discussed earlier in this chapter, there will be two judgments; one for the saved and one for the lost. Certain conditions that will prevail at one will also exist at the other. Specifically, this judgment in Daniel 7:9-12 is the Great White Throne Judgment of the lost that is described in Revelation 20:11-15. Daniel clarifies this point for us in Daniel 7:22:

"Until the Ancient of Days came, and judgment was given to the saints of the Most High; and the time came that the saints possessed the kingdom."

Occasionally, some noted Nazi leader will be captured and brought to trial for the heinous crimes that he had committed over four decades ago! But had his victims, or their friends, or their families, forgotten those terror-ridden days? No! They crowd the courtroom, throng the streets leading to the place of trial, and they loudly cry for vengeance. Even so shall it be in the day of the judgment of those who cruelly mistreated the saints of those he thought were forever dead. He will hear the recounting of sins he perpetrated in the distant past from lips he thought had been eternally silenced in death. But no, here on the witness stand of all the ages, he is held responsible for his vile acts and brutal deeds!

In Daniel 7: 10, two groups are seen as present at the Great White Throne Judgment. Every person who has ever lived, or shall yet live, will be in one of the set two groups. ". . . *A thousand thousands ministered unto him . . .* " is a reference to all of the redeemed of God who will sit with Him at the eternal judgment bar; . . *ten thousand times ten thousand. . .* "is a reference to the lost masses of unregenerated mankind, standing in hopeless dejection, waiting for the final statement of sentence from the throne: *"Depart from me, ye cursed, into everlasting fire, prepared for the devil and his angel)* (Matthew 25:41).

Please mark an unalterable fact, verse 10 states that *"The judgment was set. . .* "There will be no cancellation! Then will be no postponement! How I wish that we could somehow
get every person to realize that there will be no avoiding time of judgment!

The final phrase in verse 10 is repeated in Revelation 20:12, ". . . and the books were opened. . . '.' More will be said of this phrase when we finally arrive at the twelfth chapter I Daniel. Suffice it to say at this point, however, that there will be a full and authoritative documentation provided at the judgment. The following passages lend support to the doctrine of remembrance of the ways of man:

"Then they that jeared the Lord spoke often one to another, and the Lord hearkened, and heard it. and a book remembrance was written before him for them that feared the Lord, and that thought upon his name. And they shall be mine, saith the l.oni of hosts, in that day when I make up my jewels; and I will spare them, as a man spareth his own son that serveth him. Then shall ye return, and dist-em between the righteous and the wicked. between him that serveth God and him that serveth him not" (Malachi 3:16-18).

Behold it is wntten unto me; I will not keep silence, but will '"~'°'"P¢tI-1:8. even recompense Into their bosom, your iniquities And the iniquities of you fathers together, saith the Lord, who have burned incense upon the mountains, and blasphemed me upon the hills; there/'ore will I measure their former work into their bosom "(Isaiah 65:6-7).

He that rejecteth me, and receiveth not my words, hath one that judgeth him: the word that I have spoken, the same shall judge him in the last day. (John 12:48)

The antichrist will not succeed! He is the "*horn*" about whom Daniel 7:1 l speaks. His "great words" are no match for the words of God as indicated in the verses just quoted. It must have gladdened the heart of the prophet as he saw the antichrist defeated at the Battle of Armageddon (Revelation 19) and cast into the lake of fire (Revelation 19:20). But verse 12 of the seventh chapter of Daniel gives us a picture of the other of the world's governments that had been deceived by the antichrist. After his demise, they enter the Millennial Kingdom of Christ to continue their existence for one thousand years under His righteous rule and the authority of the saints.

In the order of events of prophecy, the Millennial Kingdom will follow the Great White Throne Judgment. So, in logical sequence, Daniel 7:14 shares simply:

> *"And there was given him (Christ) dominion, and glory, and a kingdom, that all people, nations, and languages should serve him; his dominion is an everlasting dominion, which shall not pass away, and his dominion that which shall not be destroyed."*

Daniel 7:13-14 should be read as a parallel and companion passage with Revelation 5:1-14, which gives a dramatic view of heaven.

There is, in the modem religious world, a widespread confusion about the promises made to Israel in the Old Testament and whether those promises became the inheritance of the church in the New Testament because of the rejection of Christ by the Jews. A very marked difference exists between the two, but the major promises of God made to the children of Israel are still binding.

Covenant promises are of two kinds. We have unilateral covenants, and we have bilateral covenants. A unilateral covenant is not dependent upon the faithfulness of the party to whom it is offered. A bilateral covenant, on the other hand, is dependent on the faithfulness of both parties; if one of the parties violates his responsibilities in the agreement, the other party is under no requirement to fulfill his responsibilities.

The two large covenant promises of the Old Testament that deal with the Jew are the ones made to Abraham and David. The Abrahamic Covenant and the Davidic Covenant are both unilateral covenants. In other words, regardless of the successes or failures these men and their descendants may have had in adhering to God's other commandments, there were literally no commandments required of them in these two major covenants. As a result, the rejection of the messiah (Jesus Christ) did not lose for them the promises that God had made for the establishment of an everlasting kingdom. The church, therefore, has special promises from God especially for itself, but the kingdom promises are solely for the Jews and have never been revoked. These kingdom promises will find gileir fulfillment in the Millennial Kingdom of our Lord Jesus Christ.

To distinguish between the church and the kingdom may be simplified in this manner. The church is the best Biblical example of God's grace; the kingdom is God's best example of God's righteousness.

The introduction of Christ as King comes from an Old Testament reference in Zechariah 9:9 and actually occurs in Matthew 21:11.

"Rejoice greatly, O daughter of Zion; shout 0 daughter of Jerusalem; behold. thy King cometh unto thee, he is just, and having salvation; lowly, and riding upon an ass. and upon a colt. the foal of an ass" (Zechariah 9:9).

Without question, Jesus recognized His role as the King of the Jews who would one day personally usher in the Millennial Kingdom and sit on the throne of David. Just prior to His ascension back to heaven, our Lord was queried by His disciples about the coming Kingdom:

"When they. therefore, were come together, they asked of him, saying, Lord, wilt thou at this time restore again the kingdom to Israel? And he said unto them, it is not for you to know the times or the seasons, which the Father hath put in his own power!' (Acts 1:6-7).

You will note that Jesus did not challenge their question nor disagree with them. He knew that He would eventually rule in the future kingdom. At the annunciation of His birth to Mary were these words said by the angel:

"And, behold, thou shalt conceive in thy womb, and bring forth a son, and shalt call his name, Jesus. He shall be great, and shall be called the Son of the Highest; and the Lord God shall give to him the throne of his father, David" (Luke 1:31-32).

It is beyond my ability and imagination to understand how in the world there can be such misguided believers who reject the idea of the coming kingdom when this one verse alone has never been fulfilled!

When the day of that glorious millennial kingdom shall finally dawn, the curse that this old sin-drenched world has so long endured will be triumphantly lifted:

"And he shall judge among the nations, and shall rebuke many peoples;

and they shall beat their swords into plowshares; and their spears into pruning hooks; nation shall not lift up sword against nation, neither shall they lean: war anymore" (Isaiah 2:4).

"The wolf also shall dwell with the lamb, and the leopard shall lie down with the kid; and the calf and the young lion and the fatling together, and a little child shall lead them, and the cow and the bear shall feed; their young ones shall lie down together. And the lion shall eat straw like the ox. And the sucking child shall play on the hole of the asp, and the weaned
child shall put his hand on the cockatrice den "(Isaiah l 1 :6-8).

"The wilderness and the solitary place shall be glad for them; and the desert shall rejoice, and blossom like a rose . . . Then shall the lame man leap as an hart, and the tongue of the dumb sing; for in the wilderness shall waters break out, and streams in the desert" (Isaiah 35:1, 6).

"For, behold, I create new heavens and a new earth, and the former shall not be remembered, nor come into mind" (Isaiah 65:17).

Oh, Dear Reader, this will be our kingdom. It is reserved for the saints of all ages who have longed and looked for the appearing of Jesus. Even Daniel seems caught up in the thrill of it all will he announces:

"But the saints of the Most High shall take the kingdom, and possess the kingdom forever, and ever" (Daniel 7:18).

The concluding verses in the seventh chapter of Daniel (verses 24-28) concern themselves with the final treacherous three and one-half years of the tribulation under the tyrannical rule of the antichrist. But, faint not, the victory is ours!

". . : the judgment shall sit; and they shall take away his (the antichrist) dominion, to consume it and destroy it unto the end. And the kingdom . . . shall be given to the people of the
saints . . ." (Daniel 7:26-27).

These just-quoted verses express the certainty of the saved. Everything in every place around is apparently, it would seem, under the total control of the devil. But one glad day, thank _God, all of this world's resources and powers will be given into the hands of the saints when Jesus comes to reign!

Chapter Eight

The Influence of Alexander The Great

We are now entering the most controversial part of the Book of Daniel. Those who attack the inerrancy of the Scriptures use chapters eight through twelve of this book as a favorite part of their arsenal when they mock the Word of God and challenge the integrity of the Bible. But, like all of their other "contradictions," this "intellectual" presentation by those of the schools of higher criticism is not at all a problem for the sincere Bible student who approaches these passages with an open mind.

What is it that the skeptic asserts? He, with twisted delight, suggests that no reasonable man could possibly believe that the same man wrote the entire Book of Daniel. Primarily, there are two reasons given in support of this foolish position.

First, this book is a unique book in the Bible because of the languages used in the writing of it. Two major and very different languages were employed. Chapters one through seven were written in Aramaic; chapters eight through twelve were written in Hebrew. Since these languages were so skillfully penned into the complex and colorful phraseology of their respective pans, it would be virtually impossible for one man to have possessed such masterful abilities as would be necessary to write so fluently and equally well in each of these diverse tongues.

Second, as we shall see in the study of this chapter, whoever wrote the final five chapters of the book did so with considerable attention to details. Prophecies are made in such unmistakable and precise terms that it is ridiculous to presume that such statements could have been recorded so accurately except by someone who was looking back in history instead of forward into future events. So says the liberal agnostic.

It really does not matter how unbelievable any segment in the Scriptures may be, since it is God's Word, it is not required to yield itself to the rules of human reasoning. There was a time only a few years ago that I regularly repeated a popular statement of the day, "God said it, I believe it, and that settles it." But I have learned that that is simply not true. Actually, if God says it, that settles the issue for time and eternity. It is not necessary that we place ourselves in the position of defending the trustworthiness of any part of the Scriptures. It is God's Word, as all mankind will one day be forced to confess.

Nevertheless, we are always safe if we can find words from the very lips of Jesus. Let us examine two verses that will clarify the issue for us. The first verse toward which has been ascribed as the work of an imposter:

"And he shall confirm the covenant with many for one week; and in the midst of the week he shall cause the sacrifice and the obligation to cease, and for the overspreading of abomination he shall make it desolate, even until the consummation, and that determined shall be poured upon the desolate" (Daniel 9:27).

Now, watch very closely the connection that Jesus makes with this verse in His statement as shared in Matthew 24:15:

"When ye, therefore, shall see the abomination of desolation, spoken of by Daniel the prophet, stand in the holy place (whosoever readeth, let him understand)."

The question is resolved! Jesus has spoken! Our Lord, who knows O the beginning from the end and the end from the beginning, has with this one brief statement totally annihilated the brilliant essays of the scholarly critic to nothing more than the babblings of a moron! Jesus says that Daniel wrote the entire book. Let God be true and every man a liar!

Having established the complete authorship of our book, let us now turn to the eighth chapter and begin our exposition of it. It should be noted that this is the second vision of Daniel, the first having occurred in the seventh chapter. The vision in the seventh chapter came to Daniel while he was sleeping "upon his bed' in the first year of Belshazzar's reign while the vision of chapter eight came to him while he was at the palace in Shushan during the third year of Belshazzar's reign. The first was a glimpse of events leading up to the distant end-time while the second concerned itself with soon coming world powers in the form of Persia and

Greece.

In fact, it is an extraordinary bit of Bible trivia that the prophet Daniel used the very name "Grecia" (Greece) in verse 21`

"And the rough goat is the king of Grecia, and the great horn that is between his eyes is the first king . . ."

Why is this so unusual? At the time that Daniel made this prophecy, there was not a nation of Grecia or Greece! It had not yet come into existence. There was a cluster of small, very small, city-states; but these could not by any stretch of the imagination be viewed as a nation, and especially a nation with any reasonable possibility of becoming a world empire. It would be almost another four hundred years from the time of Daniel before Greece would wield the power of a world leader. As mentioned earlier in this chapter, such precise prophetic details cause the Biblical critic to scoff at anyone who would be so gullible as to believe such obvious lies. To the undaunted believer, however, this is just another of the scriptural statements that confirms the Bible's inerrancy.

This second of Daniel's visions is recorded beginning in verse three:

"Then I lifted up mine eyes, and saw, and, behold, there stood before the river a ram which had two horns; and the two horns were high, but one was higher than the other. and the higher came up last.

There is no doubt about the interpretation of this verse; in verse 20 are these words:

"The ram which thou sawest, having two horns, these are the kings of Media and Persia."

"Horn" is a favorite Biblical term for "kings." The symbolism is made clear in Revelation 17:12:

"And the ten horns which thou sawest, are ten kings . . ."

So, the ram was a symbol shared with Daniel as a representation - of a world empire, comprised of two nations, Media and Persia. Although Media was the stronger of the two nations at the first, Persia was the "*higher came up last*"(verse 3). With Persia as the driving force, the emergence of the "*ram*" on the stage of world domination changed the balances of power.

I have been seriously studying the Word of God for many years, yet I never cease to be amazed at its accuracy. Really, I should not be surprised or astonished at all. This is God's Word, it is "theopneustos"; it is "God-breathed." But we of the human family have so accustomed ourselves to making allowances for mistakes and miscues, that we have the tendency to ascribe to God's Word the same criteria by which we would Judge it if a mere man had been the author.

But the amazement that I feel when reading some section in the Scriptures that defies human logic is sweet. It reaffirms that God is true, that His Word can be trusted implicitly. There is, in our day, the pitiful but aggressive effort by many to mock the orthodox institutions that have served us well for hundreds and sometimes thousands of years. The cry is for something new. Remember this, "If it is true, it is not new; if it is new, it is not true." Disregarding the wisdom of the ages, these hyenas of a new philosophy and a new age try to discredit the credibility of the ancient. Especially are they vicious in their maniacal snarls at the integrity of the Bible. But despite their attempts to make foolish the statements found in God's Book, they are foiled again and again, reducing their foolish criticisms to the level of morons.

Why have I said these things? In Daniel 8:5 is an often viewed "me Phrase of scriptural intrigue:

"*And as I was considering, behold. an he-goat came from the west over the face of the whole earth . . .*"

Never had there been a mighty nation come from the west. Can you imagine the guffaws of historians and political scientists of Daniel's day as they read these words? Yet, as always, the fulfillment came in precise measure as the Grecian Empire rose to world supremacy. With blitzing swiftness this army of the Hellenic state followed the ingenious battle plans of its famous leader, Alexander, and nation after nation fell before its fierce onslaught.

The he-goat, then, is a reference to Greece. Let there be no question about this particular symbol, for Daniel himself interprets it for us:

"And the rough goat is the king of Grecia, and the great horn: that is between his eyes is the first king" (Daniel 8:21).

Quite clearly, we see another magnificent prophecy in this passage. Verse five tells us that the he-goat (Greece) has a *. . notable horn between his eyes."* Verse twenty-one interprets the meaning of that horn by sharing, *. . the great horn that is between his eyes is the first king. "* Who was the first king of the world-dominating Grecian Empire? As we have already said, he was none other than Alexander the Great!

But the prophecy of Greece and Alexander is not left incomplete by Daniel. Look at verse eight:

"Therefore, the he-goat waxed very great: and when he was strong, the great ham was broken, and for it came up four notable ones toward the four winds of heaven. "

What unbelievable accuracy! When Alexander, the great horn, was at the very height of his glory as world ruler, he "was broken"; that is, he died. From the pages of secular history, we are given the sad account of his passing from this life to the next.

Alexander the Great was sexually promiscuous. He fell steadily downward into the slime of moral decadence. Finally, at the age of 33, he cries because there are no more worlds to conquer. How tragic that he had been victorious over every enemy except the one that raged within himself. Morally degenerate, his body ridden with syphilis from indulgence in multiple homosexual affairs, he died.

The Biblical term for his death is appropriate. He was broken. At the end, Alexander must have realized the foolishness of his life. It is recorded that he was buried in a casket with his hands protruding through holes in either side to show that a man takes nothing with him as he leaves this life. How well his life and death underscore the words of our Lord in Matthew 16:25-26:

"For whosoever will save his we shall lose it; and whosoever will lose his life for my sake shall find it. For what is a man profited if he shall gain the whale world, and lose his own soul? Or what shall a man give in exchange for his soul?"

An interesting historical side note is. that as Alexander the Great was pushing his way across the Middle East, he came to in an would have destroyed the city were it not for the intervention of the High Priest who told him that Daniel had prophesied his greatness. The priest then read Daniel 8:8;

"Therefore the he-goat Waxed very great: and when he was Young, the great horn was broken; and for it came up four notable ones toward the four winds of heaven. "

Alexander was so impressed that he left the area without causing the utter destruction that ordinarily followed his leaving. The *"four notable ones"* historically, were his four generals who rose to power over various segments of the empire after his death. More will be said of these men when we arrive at chapter eleven of our study. For now, their names and kingdom are sufficient

(1) Cassander: Macedonia-
(2) Lysimachus: Asia Minor
(3) Seleucus: Syria; '
(4) Ptolemy: Egypt.

In verses 9-14, we have a prophecy of double reference. The initial prophecy concerns a ruler who will spring from the house of Seleucus in Syria. His name is Antiochus Epiphanes. The second and greater prophecy in the passage is of the antichrist who is to come during the future tribulation. Look at what Daniel says of Antiochus Epiphanes in verses 9-11:

"And out of one of them came forth a little horn, which waxed exceeding great, toward the south, and toward the east, and toward the pleasant land. And it waxed great, even to the host of heaven; and it cast down some of the host of the stars to the ground, and stamped upon them. Yea, he magnified himself even to the prince of the host, and by him the daily sacrifice was taken away, and the place of his sanctuary was cast down. "

What a terrible foe this Antiochus Epiphanes was to the Jew! His atrocities, his blasphemous abominations were almost beyond the realm of the believable. He actually thought of himself as God, and he presented himself as such. In fact, archaeologists have uncovered ancient coins that he had minted with this inscription, "Antiochus: God Manifested."

To antagonize him or challenge his authority was to place oneself and one's loved ones in the awful position of likely torture and death. For example, one Jewish couple followed the dictates of their faith and had their young sons circumcised. He had strictly forbade the continuance of the rite of circumcision although it was esteemed as one of the most holy of the divine commands by the Jew. For this offense, Antiochus Epiphanes ordered the two boys placed in a corkscrew and twisted until every bone in their dead bodies had been cruelly crushed. Then, adding awful insult to injuries, the remains of their precious sons were hung about the parents' necks like a bloody scarf, and they were paraded before the people.

Another Jewish father stubbornly refused to obey and circumcised his seven sons. Hearing of this father's action, Antiochus Epiphanes raged in anger and commanded that the seven lads be placed on a burning red-hot grill. He forced the grief-stricken father to watch the ugly spectacle of his sons' torturous death and then plucked his eyes out so that the last thing the poor man would ever remember seeing was the deaths of his sons.

Not only did he physically abuse the people, but even worse was the total disrespect that he displayed for Jehovah God and the things that they viewed as sanctified and holy. No spot on earth was more sacred to the Jew than the temple. And the sacrificial altar was especially revered by them for it was there that they carefully offered lambs without spot or blemish. How horrifying it must have been for these faithful Jews to watch with anguished hearts as Antiochus Epiphanes brought a hog to their holy altar and butchered and burned it there. Then, in his mad attempt to desecrate the entire temple, he took the juices that ran from the carcass of the hog on the altar and sprinkled those juices all over the walls.

This unholy man, who typifies the antichrist, had absolutely no respect for Jehovah God. He decreed that the Old Testament, which was the sole basis of holy instruction for the Jew, was not to be read. Its regulations and requirements and rituals became the objects of scorn and were outlawed, punishable by death.

But God did not fail His people, and the people did not fail their God! A rebellion against such tyranny began! Read verses 13-14:

"Then I heard one saint speaking, and another saint said unto that certain saint which spoke, how long shall be the vision concerning the daily sacrifice, and the transgression of desolation, to give both the sanctuary and the host to be trodden under foot? And he said unto me, unto two thousand and three hundred days; then shall the sanctuary be cleansed. "

I am glad that God's Word is so exact! Note again the 2300 days in verse 14. Antiochus Epiphanes had stolen his way into the 'hearts of the Jews by promising to be their protector against their numerous enemies. After gaining their confidence, he revealed the dark side of his evil personality and began his venomous rule over them in 171 B.C. Twenty-three hundred days later this bloody period in Jewish history came to an end when a courageous liberator by the name of Judas Macabees cleansed the temple for worship again.

Who was this Judas Macabees? In the long roll of Jewish deliverers and military leaders, none is more striking than Judas Macabees. His motives were always pure and unselfish. He fought for God's glory and his country's good. His unselfish devotion was equaled by his military skills. For seven years, with unflagging enthusiasm, and generalship that has never been surpassed, he led the Jews to victory.

To adequately know this remarkable man, we must go back to an aged priest by the name of Mattathias. He had been driven by the murderous Antiochus Epiphanes to the little country town of Modin. All of the villages and hamlets, as well as the more populous areas, found themselves filled with imperial officers who had been commanded to see that heathen sacrifices were duly offered by all the citizens. A brave stand was made by Mattathias.

When ordered to offer the first heathen sacrifice, he refused. When an unclean Jew, on one occasion, came to the altar to do an unholy work, Mattathias not only killed that Jew but also one of the imperial officers that had assisted him.

Calling on all the faithful to follow him, he took his five sons (John Simon, Judas, Eleazar, Jonathan) and fled into the mountains and started the fires of rebellion against Antiochus Epiphanes and his hordes.

Many who shared the feelings of Mattathias took refuge in the wilderness, but were hotly pursued by the Syrian officers, who told them to surrender or die. One bloody Sabbath day saw one thousand Jews slaughtered rather than fight on a day that was reserved exclusively for the worship of Jehovah. But after this massacre, Mattathias and his band determined to defend themselves even if it meant fighting on the Sabbath day.

This policy shift won approval by large numbers of Jews who stepped forward to involve themselves in the conflict. Mattathias died in 166 B.C. after blessing his sons and solemnly charging them to give their lives, if necessary, in defense of their faith. The leadership was conferred by him to his son, Judas, better known as Maccabaeus, hence the name, Judas Maccabees.

Judas soon proved himself a born leader. He seemed to unite within himself the faith of Abraham, the zeal of Elijah, the status of Saul, and the courage of David. He became the pride of his nation and the terror of his enemies.

In the very first year of his leadership, he rose to fame by defeating the two Syrian generals, Apollonius and Seron. Enraged at the defeat of his forces, Antiochus Epiphanes sent half of his whole army against the Jews while he went with the other half to nearby nations to collect money.

The invading Syrians were so sure of victory over the Jews that they brought slave-traders with them to buy the Jews after the battle was over. But Judas met them fearlessly. When he learned that the Syrians planned a night attack, he removed his army and attacked the main body of the Syrian troops while they slept and ambushed the returning Syrian soldiers who had found that their prey was gone.

A year passed before the Syrians came against Israel again. When they finally came, Judas soundly defeated them at Bethzur, between Hebron and Jerusalem. In full control, Judas returned to Jerusalem to cleanse the temple.

The shrubs that were growing wild in the courts were cleared away. The heathen altar was destroyed. A new altar was erected. The sacred temple furniture that had been removed by Antiochus Epiphanes was replaced. On December 25, 165 B.C., the temple was purified by the offering of a legal sacrifice upon the new altar.

Daniel, of course, was troubled by the vision that had bee given him. Pondering the meaning of all that he had seen he suddenly saw the form of a man: '

"And it came to pass, when I, even I Daniel, had seen that vision, and sought for the meaning, then, behold. there stood before me as the appearance of a man" (8:15).

I am convinced that this man was the Lord Jesus Christ. The reason, it seems to me, is quite clear. Whoever this person is, he is giving commands to high-ranking angels as evidenced in verses sixteen and seventeen. I believe the only one that could have the appearance of a man and the authority to command angels is Jesus.

We must understand this vision in terms of "prophecy of double reference." That is, here is a prophecy that will have its first fulfillment in someone who will soon appear; but will have its second and greater fulfillment in one who will come in the distant future from the time that the prophecy was given.

The soon fulfillment of this prophecy was in Antiochus Epiphanes; the greater fulfillment will be in the antichrist who is yet to come. Note carefully the time of the vision's fulfillment:

"And I heard a man's voice between the banks of Ulai, which called, and said, Gabriel, make this man to understand the vision. So he came near where I stood: and when he came. I was afraid. and fell upon my face: but he said unto me, understand, 0 son of man: FOR AT THE TIME OF THE END SHALL BE THE VISION... and he said, behold, I will make thee know what shall be in THE LAST END OF THE INDIGNA TION: for at the time appointed the end shall be . . . and IN THE LATTER TIME OF THEIR KINGDOM, when the transgressors are come to the full, a king of fierce countenance, and understanding dark sentences, shall stand up" (Daniel 8:16, 17, 19, 23).

Do you see the phrases, ". . . time of the end . . ., " and ". . . Last end. . ., " and . . the latter time. . ."? Those are descriptive ways of pinpointing the end of the world when Jesus comes. Whenever you see that terminology, whatever prophecy is connected with it can be understood as end-time prophecy.

Several important facts may be gleaned from these verses about the antichrist. First, look at verse 23:

"And in the latter time of their kingdom , when the transgressors are come to the full, a king of fierce countenance, and understanding dark sentences, shall stand up. "

Already, in this verse, we have a chilling revelation that the antichrist will be a man of evil resources. The fact of his *"fierce countenance"* makes him a man to fear. His understanding of *"dark sentences"* places him in the domain of the demonic spirit world. How dreadful it would be if this were the only verse about him!

But there is more! His twisted character and thirst for power will finally propel him to the very top of world domination:

"And his power shall be mighty, but not by his own power: and he shall destroy wonderfully, and shall prosper, and practice, and shall destroy the mighty and the holy people" (8:24).

There are five aspects of the life and works of the antichrist given in this verse:

(1) HE WILL HAVE SUPERNATURAL POWER ". . . *and his power shall be mighty, but not by his own power. . .* "Just like Jesus was God in the flesh, the antichrist will be Satan in the flesh. He will be the devil incarnate like Jesus was God incarnate. Look at one statement about the antichrist in Revelation 13:2 that confirms the source of his strength:

"And the beast which I saw was like unto a leopard, and his feet were as the feet of a bear, and his mouth as the mouth of a lion: and the DRAGON GAVE

HIM HIS POWER, AND HIS SEAT AND GREAT AUTHORITY."

How can I be sure that this dragon is the devil? All I need to do is turn to Revelation 12:9:

"And the great dragon was cast out, that old serpent. called the devil, and Satan, which deceiveth the whole world: he was cast out into the earth. and his angels were cast out with him."

Satan will invest all of his power and fury into the life of the antichrist. It is no wonder that the world will be convinced that this will have all the answers for the woes of the nations. He will have the demonic seductive power of hell energizing him. John well describes the sinister ability of Satan to deceive:

"Ye are of your father the devil, and the lusts of your father ye will do. He was a murderer from the beginning, and abode not in the truth, because there is no truth in him. When he speaketh a lie, he speaketh of his own: for he is a liar. and the father of it" (John 8:44).

The panoramic view of the administration of the antichrist can be clearly seen in verse 25:

"And through his glory also he shall cause croft to prosper in his hand; and he shall magnify himself in his heart, and by peace shall destroy many: he shall also stand up against the Prince of princes; but he shall be broken without hand."

The initial revelation of the antichrist will not be that of a hideous, unscrupulous despot. No, a cool glass of lemonade makes a perfect cover for the murder of man in intense thirst. Simply add a little arsenic of lead and the deed is done. The calculating and cunning murderer would never hand his intended victim a bottle clearly marked with the label of arsenic of lead. The best lie is the lie veiled in truth.

When the antichrist makes his first appearance on the stage of international politics, he will do it with the fanfare and charisma of a thousand actors. With charm and superior intelligence he will win the world to his favor.

Such universal support for one man's policies will be unprecedented in the recorded history of man.

But there is an ominous "fly in the ointment." This antichrist will begin to . . *magnify himself in his heart.* " His confidence soaring on the eagle wings of public opinion will give him his false sense of destiny. Many have been the rulers of the past who accomplished so much so quickly that a greedy notion of "divine rights" began to course its way into their hearts. And as surely as proud Nebuchadnezzar was driven into humility, even so these arrogant bearers of covetousness were, in process of time, left in the ditch of historical litter.

Oh, how badly the world cries for peace. It is ready for any man who has a plan by which nations will put aside their weapons of war. Eagerly the masses will reach for this charming innovator and planner of peaceful co-existence between enemy countries. His proposal for world peace will be readily accepted and he will be elevated to a position of world leader.

Be ever on guard against any movement that smacks of any form of ecumenicism, or organizations under an inter- national umbrella. Whenever amalgamations of this sort occur, It always happens at the expense of the participating groups giving up certain distinctive powers and policies. This will provide the antichrist with easy access to the control of churches, educational institutions, and governmental bodies. Indeed, ". . . *by peace he shall destroy many.*"

At the height of his grandeur, he will make a mistake that will cost him everything. We will see this in more detail later in this study. but very simply, he will desecrate the rebuilt temple in Jerusalem' presenting himself as God. That one act will his doom. The account of this episode with applicable bible passages, as mentioned earlier, will be in entirety later.

This temple desecration will merely set the stage for his conflict with Jesus at the Battle of Armageddon: ". . . he shall also stand up against the Prince of princes . . . " Men will bow before the beast in fear, nations will cower in terror, but Jesus will defeat him. Where the hand of man with the most modern of military devices will not be able to overthrow the antichrist, Jesus will easily dispose of him. That is the meaning of the phrase, . . . shall be broken without hand. "

Such sobering information was too much for Daniel to handle He was so sensitive to God that these thoughts sickened him. Would It not be a good thing for the Christian community if we could somehow shake ourselves from the cobwebs of complacency to a holy fear of God's Word? Man, even saved man, has so little regard for the true impact of God's Word that he scarcely flinches or beads droplets of sweat when hearing of hell or the future wrath of God. Oh, if we could only be like Daniel:

"and the vision of the evening and the morning which was told is true; wherefore shut thou up the vision; for It shall be for many days. And I Daniel fainted, and was sick certain days; afterward I rose up, and did the king's business, but none understood it." (8:26-27)

Chapter Nine

The Seventy Weeks Of Daniel

This ninth chapter of the Book of Daniel is one of the most controversial passages in the Old Testament. For its position as a point of division among the true Bible scholars and those who presume to be scholars, this chapter ranks with the first eleven chapters of Genesis. How one interprets the seventy weeks of Daniel will reveal whether the interpreter is liberal or conservative in his Biblical philosophies; it will mark his general perception of the study of the Book of Revelation as premillennial, post millennial, or a millennial. This chapter, then, is crucial to much of the scriptural material that must be understood.

I think that it is interesting to note that although Daniel seemed to have a special direct connection with the Lord through which he was given divine information by visions, dreams, or astute bits of wisdom, he nevertheless exemplified himself as a man of God because of his attention to written Scriptures. Think of it! This pivotal prophecy came to Daniel as a result of his willingness to apply himself to a study of the Word!

One of the most discouraging aspects of my work as a pastor has been the general neglect of serious Bible study by the congregations of the various churches in which I have ministered. Enthusiasm for musical presentations, recreational activities, small group social excursions, and denominational concerns is more easily generated than enthusiasm for Bible preaching and teaching. The level of Bible knowledge is so low in most churches that it is almost non-existent and is virtually useless. Why should we wonder at the lack of power demonstrated by numberless local churches in numberless communities across America? We have only two spiritual weapons that are "*mighty to the pulling down of strongholds.*" I am thoroughly convinced that the man who gives little time to discovering the truths of God's Word will likewise give little time to God in prayer. One of the major reasons for Daniel's power in his prayer closet was his diligence in his study of the Scriptures.

In Daniel 9:2, the prophet's interest in study is revealed:

"In the first year of his reign I Daniel understood by books the number of

the years, whereof the word of the Lord came to Jeremiah the prophet, that he would accomplish seventy years in the desolation: of Jerusalem."

Is it not exciting that we can read the very same words that Daniel read? God used the statement of Jeremiah in his book, chapter 25, verse 11-12, to open the mind of Daniel later to a special truth. Jeremiah said:

"And this whole land shall be a desolation, and an astonishment; and these nations shall serve the king of Babylon seventy years. And it shall come to pass, when seventy years are accomplished, that I will punish the king of Babylon. and that nation, saith the Lord, for their iniquity, and the land of the Chaldeans, and will make it perpetual desolations."

We have already discussed in this study why the children of Israel were carried away into captivity for seventy years by Babylon. The southern kingdom, Judah, felt the full force of God's judgement because of their failure to let the land rest every seventh year. God gave the number of years of the captivity to Jeremiah and Daniel benefited from that revelation because he took the time to read Jeremiah's writings.

Daniel 9:3-4 shares something of his devotional times:

"And I set my face unto the Lord God, to seek by prayer and supplications with fasting, and sackcloth, and ashes: and I prayed unto the Lord my God, and made my confession, and said, 0 Lord, the great and dreadful God, keeping the covenant and mercy to them that love him, and to them that keep his commandments."

Daniel "... *set his face unto the Lord God* ..." How easy it is to be distracted by events in the world around us as we begin to pray! Moments of prayer and Bible study become the object of Satan's scorn and he will cunningly devise ways to interrupt us and draw our attention from the things eternal.

A common experience for regular prayer warriors is the frustration of interruption. A telephone will ring, someone will knock at the door, disturbing thoughts will enter the mind. It has been my observation that such demonic obstacles are most frequent and severe when I am at the threshold of some bold personal commitment. Recognizing that to be so, I can now almost gauge my devotion's power by the hindrances that accompany it.

So, like Daniel, I must enter my quiet time with the Lord with a "set" face. I purpose that I will let absolutely nothing deter me from the completion of my mission of prayer. As I have studied the lives of the heroes of the faith, that one common characteristic can always be found. They refused to put time with God in a place of secondary importance. George Mueller of England, for example, refused to do anything at all in the Performance of his daily responsibilities until he could Emerge from his morning devotional time with a heart of rejoicing over every situation in his life.

"But, you say, "If I followed the pattern of George Mueller, I would never be able to get everything done that I am required to do each day!" My friend, God is far more concerned with the quality of what we do than the quantity of what we can do. Did He not say as much in I Corinthians 3:13 as a part of the discussion of the believer's judgement?

"Every man's work shall be made manifest: for the day shall declare it. because it shall be revealed by fire; and the fire shall Try every man s work OF WHAT SORT IT IS. "

I do not believe that God is honored by the frenetic hustle-and-bustle of the modern saint. My wife has a favorite saying, "If the devil can't make you bad, he will make you busy." Most believers would never do those things that are obviously bad over those things that are good, but we are woefully guilty of doing many good things instead of performing a few best things. Good things can re-focus the mind of the praying believer from concentration on the best things.

It is not enough to have a "set" attitude in prayer. Multitudes of people in pagan faiths and false religions are rigid, more so than those of us who are Christians, in the daily ritual of their prayers. Daniel's face was . . set unto the Lord God . . . "This was no daily obligation to the prophet, some sort of perfunctory duty done in a mechanical manner. He wanted to know God! In fact, verse three says of him that "*I set my face unto the Lord God, to seek by prayer"* . . In his study of Jeremiah's writings, I am quite sure that Daniel had also read these words:

"For thus saith the Lord, that after seventy years be accomplished at Babylon I will visit you, and perform my good word toward you, in causing you to return to this place. For I know the thoughts that I think toward you, saith the Lord. thoughts of peace, and not of evil, to give you an expected end. Then shall ye call upon me. and ye shall go and pray unto me, and I will hearken unto you. AND YE SHALL SEEK ME. and find me, when ye shall search for me with all your heart' (Jeremiah 29:10-13).

In Daniel 9:4-19, we have recorded for us his prayer of intercession for the Jewish nation. His first concern was his own personal purity:

"And I prayed unto the Lord my God, AND MADE MY C ONFESSI ON, and said, O God. The great and dreadful God, keeping the covenant and mercy to them that love him, and to them that keep his commandments" (verse 4).

Daniel was fully aware that sin blocks God's ability to answer. The principle of Psalm 66:18 was one with which he was very familiar:

"If I regard iniquity in my heart, the Lord will not hear me."

Now remember, this was one of the outstanding men of God in the Bible who prayed for forgiveness. If there ever lived a man of holiness in his daily walk, it was Daniel. Yet, he would not rely upon his personal piety. He would not chance his relationship to God to the possibilities of his mind and human recall. He demanded for himself absolute certainty that all was well between him and God.

It is important to note that in verse three he had sought the Lord and in verse four he made his confession. This is the order that must always be followed. Why? Very simply, the mind of man refuses to uncover the hidden sins of the heart and unveil them to the cold light of their ugliness. Therefore, the believer must ask the Spirit of God to turn His illuminating light upon the darkness within himself and reveal the sins tucked away in his nature of carnal humanity. Nothing can escape the search- light of the Spirit's penetration and examination!

After his personal confession, Daniel began his prayer for his people.

Read it very carefully! Although this was one of the most Godly men of the Bible, he identified himself with his people as a sinner. Being the man that he was, there is no question that he was sickened by the wickedness of the Jews. In lus heart, he knew that God would be justified in the destruction of them all. Yet, he refused to separate himself from them. Like Moses, he desired to be counted with his kindred, even in the face of possible judgment from the Lord.

It is that kind of identification that produces results in intercessory prayer. If you are a sincere, Spirit-filled believer who is forced to associate with those in open rebellion against God, you must identify with them if you are to lead them to the Lord. It maybe your family, your church, or your nation, but Your responsibility of intercession for them also includes your responsibility of identification with them. In this rather lengthy prayer, please note the number of times that Daniel used personal pronouns in second-person plural form to establish himself as one of them. To aid you, I have capitalized those pronouns:

"WE have sinned, and have committed iniquity, and have done wickedly, and have rebelled, even by departing from thy precepts and from thy judgments, neither have WE hearkened to thy servants the prophets, which spake in thy name to OUR kings, OUR princes, and OUR fathers, and to all the people of the land. O Lord, righteousness belongeth unto thee, but unto US confusion of faces. as at this day; to the men of Judah, and to the inhabitants of Jerusalem, and unto all Israel, that are near, and that are far 01],' through all the countries whither thou hast driven them, because of their trespass against thee. O Lord, to US belongeth confusion of face, to OUR kings, to OUR princes, and to OUR fathers. because WE have sinned against thee. To the Lord OUR God belong mercies and forgivenesses though WE have rebelled against him; neither have WE obeyed the voice of the Lord OUR God, to walk in his laws, which he set before US by his servants the prophets. Yea, all Israel have trangressed thy law, even by departing, that they might not obey thv voice; therefore, the curse is poured upon US, and the oath that is written in the law of Moses the servant of God, because WE have sinned against him. And he hath confirmed his words, which he spake against US, and against OUR judges that judged US, by bringing upon US a great evil; for under the whole heaven hath not been done as hath been done upon Jerusalem. As it is written in the law of Moses, all this evil is come upon US, yet made WE not our prayer before the Lord OUR God, that WE might turn from OUR iniquities, and understand thy truth. Therefore hath the Lord watched upon the evil, and

brought it upon US. Fort he Lord OUR God is righteous in all his works which he doeth: for WE obeyed not his voice. And now, 0 Lord, OUR God, that hast brought thy people forth out of the land of Egypt, with a mighty hand, and hast gotten thee renown, as at this day; WE have sinned; WE have done wickedly. O Lord, according to all thy righteousness, I beseech thee, let thine anger and thy fury be turned away from thy city Jerusalem. thy holy mountain: because OUR sins, and for the iniquities of our fathers, Jerusalem and thy people are become a reproach to all that are about us" (9:5-16).

What an example of identification with erring loved ones was left for our consideration by Daniel! It is this same kind of spirit, magnified beyond our ability to measure, that brought Jesus from His place of exaltation in heaven to earth in the body of a man. While we are indeed exhorted to separate ourselves from the sins of man, we must be careful that we never lose the capacity of loving him in spite of his sins.

If you will look again at Daniel's prayer, you will see four harsh disciplinary ways with which God dealt with His people. We need to let these ways become vivid reminders that the Lord will not tolerate waywardness. In order to humble their arrogant hearts, God employed as measures of correction:

(l) Chastisement (verse 7);
(2) Confusion (verse 8);
(3) Cursing (verse ll);
(4) Confirming (verse 12).

Let us now review Daniel's intercessory prayer. First, he sought the Lord. Second, he confessed his own individual sins. Third, he identified himself with his sinning brethren.

The actual process of intercession cannot become a reality until these first three conditions have been faithfully met. Having accomplished these, however, Daniel had placed himself in a perfect position to receive an answer from the Lord.

In verses 17-19, Daniel's request before the Lord is presented. I want you to notice that not one time did he attempt to justify the sinful actions of the people. Also, a good lesson for the modem believer is that he did not try to bargain with God. You will not find Daniel saying, "*Oh God, if you will just get us out of: this mess, I promise to go to church every Sunday, read my Bible every day, and tithe my income!* " No man has ever gotten a thing from the Lord by bargaining with Him,

Mankind cannot be trusted in his agreements with God. The record of Old Testament covenants and the flippant violation of vows made before the Lord as well as the witness of "fox-hole promises" have placed mankind outside the realm of trustworthiness that would be necessary to strike a deal with God.

Instead, if we would receive good things from the Lord, we must follow the same path as that of Daniel:

(1) Seek the Lord;
(2) Repent of sins;
(3) Identify with our loved ones;
(4) Place ourselves completely upon His mercy.

Read the final segment of his prayer in verses 17-19 and note two things. He does not bargain with God, and he calls for deliverance because of the integrity of the Lord's name, sake, and mercy:

"Now therefore, O our God, hear the prayer of thy servant, and his supplications, and cause thy face to shine upon thy sanctuary that is desolate, FOR T7-IE LORD 'S SAKE. O my God, incline thy ear, and hear; open thine eyes, and behold our desolations; and the city which is called by thy name: F OR WE DO NOT PRESENT OUR SUPPLICA TTONS BEFORE THEE FOR OUR RIGHTEOUSNESS, BUT FOR THY GREATMERCIES. O Lord. hear: O Lord, O Lord forgive, O Lord hearken and do; defer not, FOR THINE OWN SAKE. O my God: for thy city and thy people are CALLED BY THY NAME. "

As a result of such intense prayer, Daniel was visited by the archangel, Gabriel, and given one of the Bible's most extraordinary prophecies. A side note to the account concerns the timing of this angelic visit. Read verse 21:

"Yea, whiles I was speaking in prayer 'even the man Gabriel whom I had seen in the vision at the beginning, being caused to fly swiftly. touched me about

the time OF THE EVENING OBLATION. "

To paraphrase a bit, Daniel was in church on Sunday night. Some of the greatest movements of God that I have ever encountered took place during the evening service on the Lord's Day. In a good, Bible-centered church, it seems to me that the morning worship service simply sets the mood for the entire day, and when night time finally comes, the gathered saints are in a state of divine expectancy. The person 'who attends in the morning but opts not to attend at night is an individual who is attempting to exist on the froth of formalism instead of the substance of the Scriptures, and it cannot be done!

Gabriel shared an important truth in verse 23. He said:

- *"At the beginning of thy supplications the commandment came forth, and I am come to shew thee, for thou art greatly beloved: therefore understand the matter; and consider the vision."*

Did you notice that the answer came at the beginning of Daniel's supplications? As soon as Daniel had sought the Lord, confessed his sins, and identified with his people, the Lord heard his prayer and set the processes in motion that would ultimately answer his prayer. What a lesson! Because he had gotten his heart right with God, the answer was granted before he even finished his prayer! Dear Reader, be well assured that God is far more concerned with where you are with Him than He is with what you need Him or can do for Him.

Now, before I share the interpretation of the seventy weeks, I want you to read it as given in the Scriptures:

"Seventy weeks are determined upon thy people and upon thy holy city, to finish the transgression, and to make an end of sins, and to make reconciliation for iniquity, and to bring in everlasting righteousness, and to seal up the vision and prophecy, and to anoint the most Holy. Know therefore and understand, that from the going forth of the commandment to
restore and to build Jerusalem unto the Messiah the Prince shall be seven weeks, and threes-core and two weeks: the street shall be built again, and the wall, even in troublous times. And alter threescore and two weeks shall Messiah be cut off but not for himself and the people of the prince that shall come shall destroy the city

and the sanctuary: and the end thereof shall be with a and unto the end of the war desolations are determined. And he shall confirm the covenant with many for one week: and in the midst of the week he shall cause the sacrifice and the ablation to cease, and for overspreading of abominations he shall make it desolate, even until the con- summation, and that determined shall be poured upon the desolate" (9:24-27).

This marvelous prophetic passage is replete with nuggets of Biblical truth. The word for "week" in the Hebrew language is "heptad," which means a unit or measurement of sevens. Sometimes it will refer to a week of years. In the story of Jacob seeking Rachel, he is told by Laban, her father, in Genesis 29:27:

"Fulfill her week, and we will give thee this also for the service which thou shalt serve with me yet another seven years."

The meaning is clear! "Week," in this incident is seven years!

The same is true in Daniel 9:24-27. Seventy multiplied by seven (the years in the "week") equals 490 years, You will note that 490 years "... *are determined upon thy people and upon thy city to finish the transgression* ..." (verse 24).

Four hundred and ninety years have been designated as the time period during which He will deal with the Jews ("*thy people*"), at *Jerusalem* ("*thy city*"). to perform six specific things in the nation of Israel. These are listed in verse 24 as the reason that there must be a seven-year period of great tribulation because these six items have not yet been accomplished. The coming tribulation, which will complete the 490 years prophesied by Daniel will:

(1) "...finish the transgression..." What is THE transgression of Israel? There are many sins that they have committed, but their sin of sins was their rejection of Jesus Christ as the Messiah. One glorious day, the house of Israel will finish that transgression and recognize Him as Lord of lords and King of kings!

(2) "... *make an end of sins* ..."A failure to accept the salvation of the Lord is the breeding ground for all kinds of evil works. These chosen people of God in Israel have been guilty of unbelievable atrocities against His blessed name,

but their desire to live for Him will cause them to find sin repulsive when they accept Him as Savior and Lord.

(3) "... *make reconciliation for iniquity*..." There is not a word in the Old Testament for "reconcile." Reconciliation is a distinctive doctrine of the New Testament, made possible by the sacrificial and atoning death of Jesus at Calvary. Finally, the nation will not only be at peaceful coexistence with God, but they will also enter a spiritual union with Him similar to that of the church.

(4) "... *bring in everlasting righteousness*..." As soon as the Jews have accepted the Lord, the seven-year tribulation period will come to a close and with it the 490-year period foretold by Daniel will also conclude. This conclusion will usher in the millennial kingdom and its rule of eternal righteousness.

(5) "... *seal up the vision and prophecy*..." One commentator has suggested that one out of three verses in the Scriptures concern themselves with the second coming of Christ. The continual strain of the Bible is that Jesus is coming! The tribulation will bring together all the visions and prophecies of His return!

(6) .. *anoint the most Holy* ... "Israel refused Jesus as their messiah almost two thousand years ago, but when he returns in glory they will respond to Him as willing subjects, place Him on the throne of David, and honor Him as King of the Jews!

Watch carefully! Daniel 9:25 says, "Know therefore and understand that FROM THE GOING FORTH OF THE COMMANDMENT T0 RESTORE AND T0 BUILD JERUSALEM ... " When did that commandment go forth? Artaxerxes made that decree to Nehemiah in the second chapter of the Book of Nehemiah. The year was 446 B.C. Remember that date; it is important.

Also in verse 25 can be found two time periods. One is "seven weeks"; the other is "threescore and two weeks." Seven weeks would be seven times seven years, or 49 years. Historically, that was the time it took to rebuild the wall of Jerusalem. After that project was successfully concluded, another threescore and two weeks (434 years) would pass before the Messiah the Prince was to be "cutoff," which is an obvious reference to the crucifixion of Christ.

If you add 49 to 434, you have 483 years. After that period of time, 483 years from the command to rebuild Jerusalem, verse 26 says that "... *shall Messiah be cut off BUT NOT FOR HIMSELF.* " The Messiah would die, but He would die for others; what a tremendous prophetic statement of Christ's substitutionary death!

The prophecy thus far is that 483 years would pass from the command to rebuild Jerusalem until the time of Christ's crucifixion. Did it happen? The command by Artaxerxes occurred in 446 B.C. Christ died in 33 A.D. Add 446 to 33 and you get 479 years. Where are the other four years? Our calendar is in error by four years. Actually, Jesus was born in 4 B.C. Now, knowing this, add 479 years to 4 years and you get 483 years, just as Daniel said. In other words, Daniel said that 483 years would transpire from the command to Nehemiah until the crucifixion; that is exactly how long it took!

But Daniel spoke of 70 weeks of years, or 490 years. We are missing seven years! Where are they? The entire 490 years comprise a period during which God has planned to deal with the Jewish nation. When the Jews rejected Christ as their Messiah, God brought His great prophetic clock to a halt at the 483 year mark. He then turned His attention to the Gentiles by providing the vehicle of the church age for their salvation. Paul spoke of this truth in Romans 11:25:

"For I would not, brethren, that ye should be ignorant of this mystery, lest ye should be wise in your own conceits; THAT BLINDNESS IN PART IS HAPPENED TO ISRAEL. UNTIL THE FULLNESS OF THE GENTILE BE COME IN"

Two important teachings are found in this verse; the Jews have been temporarily blinded, and there will be an end to the Gentile age after which the Jews will be able to "see" again. The phrase, '*fullness of the Gentiles*, " means that whenever the final person is saved during the church age according to God's sovereign plan, the saints will be removed by the rapture of the church. God will again set in motion His great prophetic clock, and the final seven years, called the "Great Tribulation," will begin.

Daniel 9:26 speaks of "... *the prince that shall come to destroy the city and the sanctuary . . .* " Who is this prince? He is the Devil Incarnate, the Beast, the Antichrist. He will be the central figure in leading the conflict against Christ during the final seven years.

That "*one week*" in Daniel 9:27 is the future period of seven years of tribulation. The antichrist will enter a peace pact with Israel, promising to be the protector, the messiah, for whom the nation has long looked. The "*midst of the week*" conforms exactly with the two three and one-half year periods in chapter eleven of Revelation in which is the account of the two witnesses sent from God:

"But the court which is without the temple leave out, and measure it not; for it is given unto the Gentiles: and the holy city shall they tread underfoot FORTY AND TWO MONTHS (346 years). And I will give power unto my two witnesses, and they shall prophecy a thousand two hundred and threescore days, clothed in sackcloth " (Revelation ll:2).

As you can see, the "*midst of the week*" of Daniel 9:27 divides the seven years of tribulation exactly as Revelation ll:2_ says that the division should be. These two chapters, one in the Old Testament and the other in the New Testament, present an insurmountable obstacle for those who would deny the existence of the tribulation week.

Daniel 9:27 also tells us that the antichrist, who will deceive the nation of Israel with his false peace pact, is destined K0 against them and . . for the overspreading of abominations he shall make it desolate . . . "Jesus spoke of this same event in Matthew 24:15:

"*When ye therefore shall see the abomination of desolation, spoken of by Daniel the prophet. stand in the holy place. (whoso readeth, let him understand:).*

What is this abomination of desolation? What is this awful deed that the antichrist will commit against Jerusalem and the people of God. Paul answers that question in his second letter to the Thessalonians:

"*Let no man deceive you by any means: for that day shall not come, except there come a falling away first, and that man of sin be revealed, thes on of perditian; who opposeth and exalteth himself above all that is called God; or that is worshipped; so that he as God sitteth in the temple of God. showing himself that he is God" (II Thessalonians 2:3-4).*

This arrogant, Satan-empowered world ruler of the end-time will move his headquarters to Jerusalem. Revealing himself to be perverted in his inward character, he will look toward the recently-constructed temple of God (built just before his ascent to power in the tribulation), and with contempt for the Lord of Glory and all things holy, this man of sin will take over the temple and pass an official declaration that he is greater than the thrice-holy God of Israel. What abomination! What desecration! Were it not for the coming of Jesus Christ in glory to put an end to this diabolical treachery, the conclusion of this world's history would be sad indeed! But, dear saint, take heart; Jesus will reign!

DANIEL

Chapter Ten

Help For The Mourning

The tenth chapter of the Book of Daniel gives us another vision of the glory of God. Almost upon every page of the Bible can be seen a portion of the total glory that is God's alone. Every bit of the human experience can be a telescope through which the magnificence of the Godhead can be enlarged. Yes, Dear Reader, you may rest assured that none of the eventualities of life is incapable of displaying at least one of the qualities Of the transcendent Lord. Even the days of despair can be indelibly marked by the renewal of some long-misplaced morsel of truth about Him that gives meaning to other will unexplainable situations.

Such is the case in this chapter. We have been privileged to stand with Daniel at the very pinnacle of human courage and personal acclaim. He has seemed invincible in confrontation! that would have utterly destroyed lesser men. His ability to remain steadfast in the face of certain death makes him a man to be admired and used as an example.

But one of the unique characteristics of the Bible is that it just as readily shows the flaws of its nobler men and women as it discusses their strengths. God's Word is not in the same mold as the revered writings of any other religious group that is in existence today. While the sacred materials of false groups " nothing more than the egotistical boastings of pseudo-religious leaders which never dare to present these men as having failed at any point in their lives, the Bible shows even its greatest characters (with the exception of Jesus) as men and women who rode the high crests of victory and walked the low road of failure. Daniel's despondency is shared in this chapter.

The hurt of Daniel is felt in verses two and three where the account is given that:

"In those days I, Daniel, was mourning three full weeks. I ate no pleasant bread, neither came flesh nor wine in my mouth, neither did I anoint myself at all. till three full weeks were fulfilled. "

This length of time should not be confused with the weeks of the previous chapter. Those weeks were weeks of years, but these are "weeks of days," or 2! days. Verse three quite clearly indicates such in that it would be absurd to presume that Daniel did not eat meat or bathe for 21 years. Also, the passage in the Hebrew literally reads, . . *weeks of days.* "

Have you ever mourned? I am not speaking of temporary sorrows and occasional times of light depression that come to all men. I am speaking of heart-rending periods when it seems your prayers are bouncing rubber-like off the gates of heaven and God seems far removed from you. Do you know that kind of ache, that kind of loneliness?

If you have been besieged with such deep anguish, then you are already well aware that Satan uses such occasions to challenge your standing with God. He hurls questions and doubts into the troubled mind with the continual taunt of, *"Where is God? You have been faithful. You have tried your best to live for Him. Now that you really need Him, where is God?"* Satan's darts sting the mind as he persistently tries to destroy the emotionally-drained and exhausted believer. Were it not for the faithfulness of the Lord in caring for His children during such dark hours, no saint would ever survive the terrible demonic onslaught that often comes to the mourning believer.

But be mindful of this! God gives Daniel a priceless gilt at the end of his fasting and mourning. He gives him His own divine presence! Oh, Dear Reader, do you see the grandeur of it all? Daniel desperately needed a word from the Lord, but he was not just given a word; he was given the Word. While all that he wanted was a reassuring statement, he got the Savior.

Is it not sweetly remarkable that we will more often have a visitation from God during the days of gloom than the days of glory, the days of sickness than the days of sunshine, the days of tragedy than the days of triumph? I will always be grateful for those times when God has come to me on some mountain peak of spiritual victory, but I hold far dearer those blessed moments of communion when the Lord has slipped silently to my side, placed His hand on mine, and whispered, "Harold, I care. "

Ah, those are the grandest of life's many essences! More than uncovering some golden Biblical truth, more than watching the movement of the Spirit among hundreds in a worship service, more, I say, more precious are the quiet times with Jesus in the parlors of pain where no other person can come to alleviate the burden.

"What a friend we have in Jesus, All our sins and grief's to bear, Mia! a privilege to carry Everything to God in prayer."

This account in the tenth chapter is a "*theophany.*" As we have shared already, this is an Old Testament appearance of the Lord Jesus Christ. Daniel sees Jesus! How in wonder he must have looked upon His dear face!

Can you imagine how Daniel must have felt as he stood before the Lord? In our day, we are witnesses to an influx of preachers, hymn writers, and dramatists who care little for the reverence due the Lord Jesus and persist in presenting him as a "good old boy."Jesus is not "the man upstairs." You are not to '*put your hand in the hand of the man who stilled the waters.*" Oh no! You are to give Him your heart! He is Lord of lords and King of kings! He is the Lamb slain from the foundation of the world.

If Jesus were to appear in physical form before you at this moment, do not think that you would vigorously shake His hand or hug His dear neck. Instead, you would fall at His blessed feet, awe-stricken at the presence of the God of glory. He is the Lord! He is the thrice-holy God of Israel! How presumptuous of us to believe that we can glibly come before Him in all of His exaltation and treat Him with the same inane chit-chat that we use so freely every day in our routine conversations with others. This spectacular presentation of Jesus is recorded in Daniel 10:5-6:

"Then I lifted up mine eyes, and looked, and behold, a certain man clothed in linen, whose loins were girded with fine gold of Uphaz; his body also was like beryl, and his face like the appearance of lightning, and his eyes like lamps of fire, and his arms and his feet in colour like to polished brass, and the voice of his words like the voice of a multitude."

Our Lord is portrayed as perfectly pure, perfectly precious —He is perfectly perfect! Words are not found in the human vocabulary, regardless of language, that can adequately describe His pristine beauty.

In the just-quoted verses, we are given a quite thorough description of Jesus:

(1) HIS BODY: "*His body also was like the beryl . . .*" Beryl is symbolic of hardness and translucency. There is no weakness in Jesus. He is totally capable of successfully meeting every challenge.

Often I have wondered about the physical form of our L..ord. When He was young and at work in His father's carpenter shop, is it possible that every time He drove a nail into wood that He was reminded of His appointment with death at the cross of Calvary?

There is a painting that I should like to own one day. Jesus is painted as a tired young lad at the end of a hard day's work in the carpenter's shop. He is seen standing in the shop's open door facing the sunset. As He wearily yawns, He stretches His arms. The sunlight casts a shadowy silhouette on the back wall of the shop. It is the shadow of the cross!

(2) HIS FACE: *. . and his face like the appearance of light*ning *. .* Have you ever looked somewhat nervously toward dark, gathering clouds? Suddenly, a jagged streak of lightning lights the sky and seems to pierce into your very heart. With an almost hypnotic spell, you find yourself unable to move as you stand there with eyes fixed on the skies, wanting but not wanting to see the lightning flash again.

So it is with the face of Jesus. A face is useful to others for only one thing. By a person's face we are able to know whether he is pleased or displeased. For those of us who are saved, we long with anticipation for the day that we shall behold Him! However, we nervously approach that day with anxiety because of the all-knowing look of Jesus that will finally fall on each of us. It is a strange combination of wanting to see, but not wanting to see, His face.

(3) HIS EYES: *. . and his eyes like lamps of fire. . .*" The sole function of

a lamp is for illumination. His eyes, according to Revelation 1:14 as well as this verse, are flames of fire that will bum through the artificial shields that we have erected to hide the secrets of our hearts. Paul told the church at Corinth that their works would be tested by fire at the judgment seat of Christ. I believe that that fire will bum straight from the eyes of Jesus. Each of us will be thoroughly scrutinized by the Lord's all-seeing gaze that will penetrate the deepest and darkest crevices of our hearts.

There are some special times in the Scriptures that I wish That I could have beheld the look in the eyes of Christ. I can only imagine the twinkle of His eyes as he lifted little tousle-haired, Dirty-faced children so tenderly onto His lap. Or, what about the look of compassion that fell from His sweet face as He touched the woman who was bowed over double in the temple? Or, what can we say of the look of total authority as He stood up in the boat on the troubled seas before His frightened disciples and commanded the winds and the waves to be still? Or, what pain there must have been in His tear-dimmed eyes as He stood before the tomb of His dear friend, Lazarus. Or, how loving must have been His tender look from the cross upon the multitudes as He besought the Father to forebear His judgment upon these poor, ignorant people. Or, what glory must have flashed from His eyes when He arose from the grave and prepared for His grand ascension back to heaven. How often I have longed to look into the eyes of our dear Savior! And one day I will!

(4) HIS ARMS AND FEET: "... *and his arms and his feet like in colour to polished brass...* " Brass, in the Bible, is a symbol of God's judgment. For example, you will recall that in the tabernacle there was a brass laver in which could be found the water that was necessary for the cleansing of the hands and feet of the priest as he went about performing his priestly functions. That brass laver, therefore, was a picture of God's judgment upon sin in the believer's life with the washing by the Word of God.

We will be judged! Make no mistake about that! Judgment is coming! He will act as the Righteous Judge before whom the huddled masses of this world must stand.

(5) HIS VOICE: "... *and the voice of his words like the voice of a multitude...* " The voice of-Christ was unlike any that had ever been heard. He

spoke with such authority that at His betrayal by Judas in the Garden of Gethsemane the Roman soldiers fell backwards when He spoke. Remember, since Jesus was God in the flesh, every word that passed between His lips was literally the Word of God. The magnificent words of Jesus were also the Words of Almighty God, therefore Hebrews 4:12 is relevant to the things Jesus said:

"For the word of God is quick. and powerful, and sharper than any two-edged sword. piercing even to the dividing of soul and spirit, and of the joints and marrow, and is a discerner of the thoughts and intents of the heart. "

Daniel 10:6 is a presentation of the just described qualities of Christ and should be read alongside Revelation 1:13-15 which is its parallel:

"And in the midst of the seven candlesticks one like unto the Son of man, clothed with a garment down to the foot, and girt about the pops with a golden girdle. His head and his hairs were white like wool, as white as snow; and his eyes were as a flame of fire; and his feet like unto fine brass, as if they burned in a furnace; and his voice as the sound of many waters. "

All of these statements about. Jesus are true, of course. But there is one special thing that is said about Jesus by the Apostle Peter that sums up my feelings almost exactly:

"Unto you therefore which believe he is precious. . . "(I Peter 2:7).

This verse, takes on added meaning when we understand that precious is more accurately translated as "*preciousness.* " Jesus is preciousness! He is the total of all that is precious! I think Charles H. Gabriel, the hymn writer, expressed the feelings of many when he penned:

"So precious is Jesus, My Saviour and King, His praise all the day long, With rapture I sing, To Him in my weakness, For strength I can cling, For He is so precious to me. . . For 'He is so precious to me., He. is so precious to me, Till heaven below, My Redeemer to know, For He is so precious to me. "

Let us now return to the tenth chapter of the Book of Daniel. Please remember that Daniel is terribly despondent For twenty-one longs days he has fasted and prayed and waited for a word from God. But why was the Lord apparently deaf to his cries? Only someone who has had a similar experience can appreciate the depth of frustration through which" Daniel was passing.

I remember. a time in my life when each morning was greeted by me with a heavy burden. Days just thudded along with nothing more than occasional intervals of fleeting happiness. Often I recall my crying out to God for relief. Where there had always been a joyous relationship of sweet communion between me and the Lord, there was now a spiritual darkness so thick that I felt that I could never penetrate it. A loneliness like I had never known covered me like a shroud. And it seemed the more desperately I needed God, the farther He was from me. Day after day, week after week, I called upon Him with no answer returning from the throne. I can remember those despairingly long weeks and relate to the dejection of Daniel here in the tenth chapter.

In the twelfth verse is found a beautiful little statement of comfort from the Lord:

"Then said he unto me, fear not, Daniel.-for from the first day that thou didst set thine heart to understand, and to chasten thyself before thy God, thy words were heard, and I am come for thy words. "

Did you see it? God said, "*. . . for from the first day . . . Thy words were heard.*" Daniel had been praying for twenty-one days, but the heavens seemed shut up to his prayers. How wrong he was! God had been tenderly listening to his plaintive plea from the very first day. It was like a breath of fresh air to the prophet to know that God had been listening all the while.

This brings us to a disturbing question. If God had been hearing Daniel's prayers from the first day, why did He wait 21 days to answer? The answer is given in verse 13:

"But the prince of the kingdom of Persia withstood me one and twenty days: but, lo, Michael, one of the chief princes, came to help me; and I remained there with the kings of Persia. "

Demonic activity had risen up as an obstacle to the answer of God to

Daniel. Does this mean that Christ is hindered so much by demons that even He must turn to military angels like Michael for assistance? No, Christ, who is omnipotent, is never hindered by Satan or any of his demonic followers, but the work of Christ can be obstructed.

Christ chooses to work through men. In this chapter, it seems obvious that our Lord intended to answer Daniel's prayers through the leadership in Persia. Note that .. *The prince of the kingdom of Persia withstood* . . ." our Lord for twenty-one days. Apparently, a vicious power struggle took place among the hierarchy of leaders in Persia.

Michael, whose name means "*who is like God,* " is summoned to enter the fray. From the Biblical references we have of Michael, it is well established that he is the angel who is in charge of heaven's defense of Israel. Is it not grand that our Heavenly Father has so delegated His angelic hosts to take control of the enemies that would harm His children? This is true of individual believers as well as nations. Consider Matthew 18:10:

"Take heed that ye despise not one of these little ones; for I say unto you, that in heaven their angels do always behold the face of my Father which is in heaven. "

Does it seem contradictory that this angel who symbolizes Jesus would find it necessary to enlist Michael for his assistance? Does this indicate that there are angels with more power than Jesus? Does it mean, as some suggest, that this passage proves that Jesus is indeed less than God since He was unable to withstand a demon spirit without support from Michael?

No, there is no such indication intended. Throughout the life and ministry of Christ, we see Him using the same method! that are available to man in His conflicts with the devil. We ought to thank Him for doing so. If Jesus had defeated Satan as God, we could not have used His ways and made them ours in our continual battles with the devil. But since He defeated Satan as man, we have the necessary encouragement and example that we may employ to utterly free ourselves Of Satanic attack.

Think of the encounter between Christ and the devil at the Mountain of

Temptation. As omnipotent God, it would have been so very easy for our Lord to completely destroy the devil

Yet, He chose for our sakes to quote from the written Word as His defense. In other words, it was the decision of Christ to defeat Satan in His humanity rather than His deity so that we would have a pattern and battle plan to use in our own spiritual conflicts.

This same principle is true in the tenth chapter of Daniel. The angel symbolizing our Lord calls upon Michael in order that we may know the power that is available to us in the arsenal of the Lord.

It is a natural inclination for us to try to explain difficulties in our lives as "accidents." For the child of God, accidents do not occur. We are daily guided into new avenues of a variety of experiences that provide golden opportunities for growth in spiritual maturity. Times of frustration will always come from one of two sources.

(1) TEMPTATION BY SATAN: Most saints find it rather simple to discern between that which is right and that which is wrong. We know right from wrong. We readily recognize obvious sin. However, the subtler forms of unrighteousness are exercised upon the believer in the guise of trying to determine that which is an opportunity from that which is a temptation.

For example, a teenager knows that it is wrong for him to stay out of school and waste the day at some place of amusement. It would be a sin for him to do so. But suppose that same teenager has no father at home and his mother suddenly becomes gravely ill and is unable to work. And suppose this teenager is offered a job at a service station pumping gasoline by which extra, and desperately needed, money could be brought into his home.

He is now faced with the possibility that this employment offer could be used to ease the pressure at home, which means that it may be considered an opportunity. On the other hand, this job venture may result in a discontinuance of his education, which means that he would have a handicapped future thereby making this immediate choice a possible temptation to do that which is not in his best interest.

What I have shown in this illustration is that daily decisions should be viewed in the realm of temptation vs. opportunity. The Bible teaches us that God never tempts man, therefore this apparently "un-religious" question that has caused this young man a problem falls out of a simple secular decision into the spiritual. How do we know that? James 1:13 tells us:

"Let no man say when he is tempted, I am tempted of God, for God cannot be tempted with evil, neither tempteth he any man."

We must not ever forget that our lives cannot be divided into religious and secular. Everything in our daily walk through the routines of life is a situation that will be met with the approval of God or the approval of the devil. At its very foundation, that is what is meant by spiritual warfare:

"For we wrestle not against flesh and blood, but against principalities, against powers, against the rulers of the darkness of this world, against spiritual wickedness in high places."

A vitally important precept for every believer to learn is that from the day of his salvation until the day of his death he will be involved, whether he recognizes it or not, in spiritual warfare with the powers of darkness. If he does not recognize it, he is backslidden and out of fellowship with God.

The victorious Christian life is not one that is marked by an absence of conflict with Satan; it is, on the contrary, a life that seems to be an almost running battle with the devil. Remember, the children of Israel never had fought an enemy while wandering in the wilderness, but when they crossed the Jordan River and entered the Promised Land, they were constantly locked in bloody wars or mild skirmishes with the Canaanites who are a type of Satan.

(2) TESTINGS BY THE SAVIOR: Another source of problems we encounter is God. Does that seem strange? It should not. By His tests, we are made stronger in the Lord.

Consider this Biblical example. When the children of Israel left Egypt, they trekked across the desert sand and finally arrived at the Red Sea. This placed them in a dilemma. They could not cross this wide and deep body of water. Pharaoh's army was rapidly giving chase behind them. What were they to do?

Was this predicament a mistake or a foolish miscalculation of routes by their leader, Moses? It was not. They were where they were because God was leading them. God knew before they ever left captivity in Egypt that He would bring them to this very point.

Why did He do it? God knew something about the Jews that they did not know about themselves. They would require an unflinching faith in His ability to care for them if they were to survive the rigors of the Land of Promise. They would be faced with the impenetrable walls of Jericho, the frightening challenge of giants, and the cruel taunts of Baal-worshipers. If they entered the Promised Land without concrete evidence that God could be trusted in His care for them, it would not be long before they would be ignominiously defeated.

The Red Sea experience, therefore, was the Israelites' opportunity to learn a valuable lesson about the Father. That lesson was a very basic one, critical to believers of all the ages of history and in all situations: *"When you find that your only hope is God, you will find that He is all you need."* What appeared as a gigantic problem became for the Jews their immediate escape and future assurance.

For Daniel, God seemed very far away. Oh, how he longed for a word from God! Past times of sweet communion could not supply his need of God in his present sorrow. Our Lord responded by sending His angel. The angels still come to the side of the troubled believer. Read with rejoicing Hebrews 1:13-14

"But to which of the angels said he at any time, sit on my right hand, until I make thine enemies thy footstool? Are they not all ministering spirits, sent forth to minister for them who shall be heirs of salvation?"

Dear Reader, do not feel destitute and estranged from God! His angels are very near! Even if you, like Daniel, are lonely and in the grip of deep, deep sorrow, the ministering spirits of God are invisibly standing guard over you. We ought to praise His name 'continually for the provision of the heavenly host as our guardians!

Not only does God send His angels as our ministering spirits to attend to our every need, but He blesses us with His tender touch that signifies His willingness to make contact with men at the point of their deepest need:

"*And, behold, an hand touched me, which set me upon my knees and upon the palms of my hands*" *(verse 10).*

Bill Gaither wrote a song only a few years ago that was destined to become an all-time favorite in the body of Christ. The title is a simple one, "*He Touched Me.*"

"*Shackled with a heavy burden, 'Neath the load of guilt and shame, Then the hand of Jesus touched me And now 1 am no longer the same. He touched me, Oh, He touched me, And oh, what joy filled my soul, Something happened, and now I know He touched me, And made me whole.*"

It must have been tranquilly comforting to be touched by the Lord Jesus Christ. What a day it must have been when Jesus Ever so gently placed His fingertips on the eyes of a blind man, or gently massaged the aching back of the woman bent double in the temple, or reached for the withered hand, or gripped the hand of the lame to pull him to his feet or playfully patted a winsome child on the head. '

The touch of Jesus conveys His compassion and under-standing; but it is also a Physical means of expressing His assurance us that all is going to be right in the end. Each believer may take considerable consolation in the touch of Christ that came with the new birth.

Verse 16 is not the only account in chapter l0 of the Lord touching Daniel. There is another verse that shares the same caring gesture of the Father:

"*And, behold, one like the similitude of the sons of men touched my lips: then I opened my mouth, and spake, and said unto him that stood beFore, O my Lord, by the vision my sorrows are turned upon me, and Y have retained no strength . . . then there came again and touched me one like the appearance of a man, and he strengthened me*" *(verses 16, 18).*

Spiritual warfare is the underlying theme of the chapter. This angel who touches Daniel is a theophany of the Lord Jesus. Primarily, we see Him as a theophany because verse 16 describes Him as, ". . . one like the similitude of the sons of men. " As Lord of Glory and Captain of the Hosts of Heaven, Jesus does battle with Satan in two dimensions.

Note the phrase in verse 13, ". . . *and I remained there with the kings of Persia.* " After the initial conflict with the demon forces who were influencing the 'leaders of Persia, this angel who represents Jesus stayed with the leaders to provide additional support and power. That being the case, we would be inclined to suppose that the demons could never again pose a serious threat to those in Persia. That is not the case at all. Christ is forced to return!

"Then said he, knowest thou wherefore I come unto thee? And now will I return to fight with the prince of Persia: and when I am gone forth, lo, the prince of Grecia shall come" (verse 20).

The lesson here is clear! Just because we are able to conquer Satan in a given situation, it does not mean that he is utterly vanquished to never again trouble us in that situation.

But the general human interest of the chapter is Daniel's emotional state. He is, in the main, unbelievably depressed. Overcome by the weariness of the heavy responsibilities of life that taxed his emotions until there was nothing left, the touch of the Master's hand, however, caused the sun in his heart to shine again:

"And said, O man greatly beloved, fear not: peace be unto you, be strong, yea, be strong. And when he had spoken unto me, I was strengthened, and said, let my Lord speak; for thou hast strengthened me" (verse 19).

Chapter Eleven

Antiochus and Antichrist

Most commentators agree that the importance of this eleventh chapter lies in verses 35-45. It is in these verses that the last world ruler is discussed. Why is it necessary to work through the first thirty-five verses in order to get to the section concerning the antichrist? It would seem that his Biblical importance would necessitate his placement at the very opening of the chapter.

The answer to that question provides us an opportunity to learn something of the desire of the heart of God to supply His children with concrete assurance that He can always be trusted. Please note that the first thirty-five verses are historical; that is, they are descriptive of events that Daniel were in the future but for us are in the past. Verses 36-45 have not yet occurred; they are all prophecies to be fulfilled in the fixture.

Therefore, what we have in this chapter is "prophecy of double reference." Prophecy of double reference is the telescoping of a greater event in the far future through a lesser event-in the near future. When the lesser event occurs just as predicted, we can have good footing for believing that the greater event will also just as accurately come to pass.

One of the Bible's best examples of "*prophecy of double reference*" is found in Matthew 24 where the Lord speaks of the Great Tribulation Period. To help his followers fully grasp the horror of those days, Jesus told them of the soon-coming destruction of Jerusalem in A.D. 70. When His disciples witnessed the fall of the city just as the Lord had told them, they recalled His words of some thirty years earlier and began to speak and write of that more awful time that still lies in the fixture.

That same device is used here in Daniel's tenth chapter. The entire region of the Middle East is seen gripped in military conflict in the first part of the chapter, finally giving rise to the fierce and bloody rule of Antiochus Epiphanes in verse 21-" Through the prophecies of the anti-Jewish sentiments Epiphanes, we have "telescoped" for us the even greater hatred for Israel by the antichrist who is yet to appear on the world scene.

Let us now turn our attention to the first section of chapter eleven by looking at this unusual prophecy:

"Also I in the first year of Darius the Mede, even I, stood to confirm and to strength him. And now will I shew thee the truth. Behold! There shall stand up yet three kings in Persia; and the fourth shall be far richer than they all: and by his strength through his richer he shall stir up all against the realm of Grecia" (1 1:1-2).

We know from secular history that Darius reigned from 521 to 484 B.C., so this means that the prophecy of this chapter has a reliable date, 521 B.C.

I think it would be interesting to share a brief thumb-nail sketch of the rule and administration of Darius so that We might better acquaint ourselves with the life and times of Daniel. Darius was a thinker; he was an innovator. For a time, his mind seemed preoccupied with the arts of peace. He built I great palace at Susa and erected magnificent edifices at Persepolis. He reformed the administration of the government, making such wise and lasting changes that he has been called the "second founder of the Persian Empire." Most notably, Darius constructed post roads with which he bound together all parts of his extended dominion. By these roads he was able to rapidly move troops, supplies, and emergency messages. The celebrated Royal Road ran from Susa through Assyrta, Armenia, and Asia Minor; it continued past Sardes and ended at the Aegean Sea at Ephesus. Over it the royal courlefe, changing frequently their mounts, carried the command! Of Darius, "swifter than the crane." This magnificent road was a main artery of ancient trade and commerce for more than e thousand years.

Upon completion of the Royal Road, Darius conceived and entered upon the execution of vast plans of conquest, the far reaching effects of which were destined to live long after he had died. He determined to extend the frontiers of his empire into India and Europe alike.

In one blow, Darius brought the region of northwestern India known as the Punjab under his authority and thus by a single effort pushed out the eastern boundary of his empire so that it included one of the richest countries in Asia.

Several campaigns in Europe followed. These brought Darius into direct contact with the Greeks. Unfortunate for him, and for his son, Xerxes I (484-464 B.C.), this meeting with the Greeks ultimately led to the fall of the Persian Empire.

From the vantage point of the first year of the reign of Darius the Great, during which Daniel gives us the prophecy of the eleventh chapter, let us look backward to three other Persian rulers who were significantly involved in the plight of the children of Israel in Babylon. This is not recorded in the Scriptures, so we must resort to ancient history for the additional facts and details of these men.

Cynis the Great (558-5 29 B.C.) assumed control over the Medes as we have already seen in our study of the ram with two horns in the eighth chapter of Daniel. He overthrew the Median chieftains and thereby assumed headship of both the Medes and the Persians. Through his energy and soldierly genius, Cynis soon built an empire more extended than any over which a scepter had been waved by any monarch before his time.

In the attempts by Cyrus to stretch the boundaries of his kingdom, he eventually came to Lydia upon whose throne sat Croesus (560-546 B.C.). The Lydian state was a vast one, and the king collected huge taxes from all the cities in the area of modern Greece. Additionally, he owned large gold mines. This combination of taxes and gold made him the richest monarch of his day, resulting in the saying "rich as Croesus."

Croesus anxiously watched the approaching army of Cyrus. Without waiting for his allies from Egypt and Babylon, Croesus crossed the Halys River to engage in battle with Cynis and the army of Persia. But he had misjudged the strength of his enemy. Cyrus defeated the Lydians and went on to capture its capital city of Sardis.

This war between Croessus and Cyrus has a special importance from the fact that it brought the Persian Empire into contact with the Greek city-states of Asia, and thus led directly to the struggle between Greece and Persia, known as the Greco-Persian War. The fall of Lydia was quickly followed by the fall of Babylon as we have previously studied in the fifth chapter of Daniel when the Babylonians' lords were feasting with their foolish leader, Belshazzar.

Tradition says that Cyrus lost his life in an expedition against Scythian tribes in the north. He was buried at Pasargadae, the old Persian capital, and there his tomb stands today, surrounded by the ruins of the magnificent building with which he adorned the city.

Cyrus the Great left two sons, Cambyses and Smerdis; the former, as the elder son, inherited the throne. He began an unfortunate reign by causing his brother, whose influence he feared, to be put to death.

With far less ability than his father for their successful execution, Cambyses conceived even greater projects of conquest and dominion. Upon a slight pretext, he invaded and conquered Egypt and Nubia. After a short and unsatisfactory stay Egypt, Cambyses began his long return trip home to Persia. While on his way, news was brought to him that his brother, Smerdis, had taken the throne. Actually, an imposter by the name of Gomates, who resembled the murdered Smerdis, had seized the kingdom through an impersonation. Entirely disheartened by this startling tum of affairs, Cambyses took his own life, having reigned from 529-522 B.C.

The Persian nobles soon realized the fakery of Smerdis, removed him from the throne and placed Darius there in his place. We have already overviewed the rule of Darius. Suffice it to say at this point, however, that his first act as king was to punish those who had aided Smerdis in his attempt to rule over Persia.

With the previous background information in mind, let us see its relevancy to Daniel 11:2:

"And now will I shew thee the truth, Behold, there shall stand up yet three kings in Persia. and the fourth shall be far richer than they all: and by his strength through his riches he shall stir up all against the realm of Greeia " (Daniel 11:2).

These four kings in verse two are:

(1) Cambyses ($29-522 B.C.); ,
(2) Smerdis (imposter) (522-521 B.C.);
(3) Darius I (521-484 B.C.);

(4) Xerxes (known as Ahaseurus in the Book of Esther) (484-465 B.C.).

Because the Persian Empire and its influence are not as well known as the Babylonian culture to the average Bible student, let us lend our attention to their religion. After all, this pagan religious tradition was one with which the prophet Daniel was forced to contend.

The literature of the ancient Persians was mostly religious. Their sacred book was called the *Zend-Avesta*. Their religious system, as taught in the *Zend-Avesta*, was Zoroastrianism, from Zoroaster, its founder. This great reformer and teacher lived and taught about 1000 B.C.

Zoroastrianism, the first religion that claimed to be universal, was a system of beliefs best defined as dualism, with a good spirit and a bad spirit. The good spirit was named Ahura Mazda whose emblem was fire. Upon high mountain tops the eternal flame on fire altars was kept burning from generation to generation. Because of their obsession with fire, the Persians are often called fire worshippers.

Opposed to the good spirit was the evil spirit, Akriman, who was constantly striving to destroy the good creations of Ahura by creating all the evil things-storms, droughts, pestilences, wild animals, weeds, and thorns with the inward heart of man filled with evil thoughts. From the beginning of eternity, these two powers had been able to take a decided advantage. But the Persians believed that in the near future the good spirit, Ahura, would triumph over Akriman, the bad spirit, and evil would be forever destroyed.

The duty of man was to aid Ahura by working with him against the evil Akriman. He must labor to eradicate every evil and vice from his own heart, to reclaim the earth from barrenness, and to kill all noxious animals—frogs, toads, snakes, lizards-which Akriman had created. The ancient historian Herodotus watched with amazement the Persian priests as they engaged themselves in slaying these kinds of animals in a "pious pastime." Agriculture was a sacred calling because the farmer was reclaiming the ground from the curse of the dark spirit.

The curse of the ground by the evil spirit caused the Persians an unusual problem. What was to be done with the dead bodies of the people? How were they to be disposed? They could not be burned because of their worship of fire. They could not be buried because of their belief that the ground was cursed. Likewise, the bodies could not be thrown into the sea because of a curse upon the water. Since air was worshiped, the body could not be left in a tomb or in open air to decay. So, the bodies were fed to birds and wild beasts. Most often this was accomplished by exposing them on lofty towers in isolated areas. Those whose feelings would not allow them to use such ways to dispose of their dead were permitted to bury them, provided they first encased the body in wax to permanently separate it from the air and the ground.

In ancient Egypt, their moral feelings caused them to include an eternal judgment in their Osirian religion; in like manner the Persians also created a judgment of the dead. Their concept, however, was higher and loftier than that of the Egyptians. The soul was conceived as being judged by itself. Upon its departure from this life, the soul of the faithful was met by a beautiful maiden, *'fair as the fairest thing,"* who said to him: "*I am thine own conscience; I was lovely and thou madest me lovelier; I was fair and thou modest me still fairer through thy good thought, thy good speech, and thy good deed.*" And then the soul was led into the paradise of endless light. But the soul of the wicked one was met by a hideous old woman, "*uglier than the ugliest thing,*" who was his own conscience. She said to him: "*I am thy bad actions, 0 youth of evil thoughts, of evil words, of evil deeds, of evil religion. It is an account of thy will and actions that I am hideous and vile.*" And then the soul was led down into the hell of endless darkness. Thus in the earliest period of the faith of the Zend-Avesta was taught the doctrine that heaven and hell are within the human soul itself, and that conscience is the supreme witness and judge of the soul's worthiness or unworthiness.

Although the religion of the Persians was pagan and contrary to the God of Israel, one of their special and hallowed virtues of their moral code was truthfulness. As Ahura was the god of sincerity and truth, the man who battles on his side must also be sincere and truthful. Lying was a capital crime. To lie, to deceive, was to be a follower of Akriman, the god of lies and deceit. "*The most disgraceful thing in the world,*" says the ancient historian Herodotus in his account of the Persians, "*they think, is to tell a lie.*" In this report on the Persian system of education he says, "*The boys are taught to ride, to draw the bow, and to speak the truth.*" Included in the record of many Persian officials is the statement, "*I was not wicked, nor a liar.*" The Persian rulers, who shamed all other nations both ancient and modem, sacredly kept their pledged word.

This may seem to have been a rather lengthy commentary on verse two of the eleventh chapter of Daniel, but I think it is important so that you may get something of the flavor of the times during which Daniel lived. Those were exciting days that the world will never see again! Men like Darius were live, flesh-and-blood men. By learning about them, we can appreciate the challenges that faced the heroes of the Bible even more.

Now, we move to prophecies in chapter eleven of another nation. After Persia, our attention is shifted to Greece in verses three and four:

"And a mighty king shall stand up, that shall rule with great dominion, and do according to his will. And when he shall stand up, his kingdom shall be broken, and shall be divided toward the four winds of heaven; and not to his posterity, nor according to his dominion which he ruled: for his kingdom shall be plucked up, even for others beside those."

Historically, we know that the nation that replaced Persia in world domination was Greece. The "great king" of verse three is a reference to Alexander the Great.

In the spring of 334 B.C. Alexander led his army of thirty-five thousand men into a course of battles that he hoped would finally end in victory over the Persian Empire. At the Battle of Issus in 333 B.C., at the northeast corner of the Mediterranean Sea, he met and defeated the Persian army of over six hundred thousand men. The king of Persia, Darius III (336-3 30 B.C.), escaped and fled to his capital city of Susa to raise another army to oppose the march of his conqueror.

After successfully defeating Tyre (332 B.C.), Alexander turned toward the Egyptians who made no resistance to his advances. Even in those ancient days, news traveled fast. Egypt had heard of Alexander's crushing victories at Issus and Tyre and his exploit with the Gordian knot in Phrygia.

Legend has it that in the temple at Phrygia was a chariot at the pole of which was a yoke fastened by a curiously intricate knot. Word had been spread abroad that whoever could untie the knot would become master of all Asia.

Alexander attempted the feat. Unable to loosen the knot, he drew his sword and cut it Hence, we were given the phrase, "cutting the Gordian knot, " meaning a short way out of a difficulty and named for the city of Gordium in Phrygia.

While in Egypt, Alexander founded at one of the mouths of the Nile a city that he named for himself, Alexandria. Rapidly, this city became a leader in world commerce and as such attests to the farsightedness of its founder.

From Egypt, Alexander retraced his steps to Syria and marched eastward. At Arbela, not far from the ancient city of Nineveh, he met the re-gathered army of Persia under the leadership of Darius III whom he had earlier defeated at Issus. This vast army of over one million men was literally slaughtered on the battlefield of Alexander's army. Again, Darius fled the field as he had done at Issus, but was later treacherously killed by one of his own men.

Much more could be said of Alexander's other triumphs that followed his conquest of Persia. For this study it is not necessary to detail his successes at Babylon, Susa, Persepolis, Bactria, and Sogdiana; or of his often overlooked rediscovery of the sea route from the Indus to the Enphrates. These remarkable conquests had important and far-reaching consequences. First, they ended the long struggle between Persia and Greece, and that spread the Hellenic civilization over Egypt and western Asia.

Second, the distinction between Greek and barbarian was obliterated, and the sympathies of men, hitherto so narrow and local, were widened, and thus an important preparation was made for the reception of Christianity.

Third, the world was given a universal language of culture, which was a further preparation for the spread of Christ's teachings.

This influence of the Greeks was especially great in terms of molding religious concepts that affected those who lived in Israel during the time of Christ.

The early Greeks supposed the earth to be, as it appears, a plane, oval or circular in form like a shield. Around it flowed the "*mighty strength of the ocean river,* " a stream broad and deep, on the far side of which lay realms of darkness and terror. The heavens were a solid vault, or dome, the edge of which shut down tight upon the earth. Beneath the earth, reached by subterranean passages was the realm of Hades, the place of departed souls. Still beneath this was the prison Tartaws, a pit deep and dark, made fast by strong gates of brass and iron.

The sun was an archer god. borne in a fiery chariot up and down the steep pathway of the skies. Naturally it was imagined that the regions in the extreme east and west, which were bathed in the near splendors of the sunrise and the sunset, were lands of delight and plenty. The eastern region was the favored country of the Ethiopians, a land which even Zeus himself so loved to visit that often he was found absent from Olympus when sought by people praying to him. In the western region, adjoining the ocean, were the Isles of Blest, the home of heroes and poets.

These early Greeks believed in a twelve-member council comprised of six gods and six goddesses. The male deities

(1) Zeus: the father of gods and men;
(2) Poseidon: ruler of the sea;
(3) Apollo: god of light, music, and prophecy;
(4) Ares: god of war;
(5) Hephaestus: god of fire and thunderbolts;
(§) Hermes: god of wind and the swift-footed herald of the celestials, the inventor of the pipe and lyre for "the wind whistles and sings. "

'On the other side were the equally important female deities, or goddesses:

(I) Hera: the proud and jealous queen of Zeus;
(2) Athena, sometimes called Pallas: the goddess of wisdom and patroness of the domestic arts who sprang full- grown from the forehead of Zeus;
(3) Artemis goddess of the chase;
(4) Aphrodite: goddess of love and beauty, born of the white sea foam;
(5) Hestia: goddess of the hearth;
(6) Demeter: goddess of grains and harvests.

Besides these great gods and goddesses, there was an almost infinite number of other deities. These deities, great and Not so great were simply magnified human beings. They often gave way to fits of anger and jealousy. They were capable of the full range of human emotions. For example, the entire celestial council, at the sight of Hephaestus limping across the palace floor, burst into "*inextinguishable laughter*"; and Aphrodite, weeping, moved everyone to tears. They surpassed mortals in power rather than in size of body. They were able to render themselves visible or invisible to human eyes. Their food was ambrosia and nectar; their movements were swift as light. They suffered pain; but death could never come to them, for they were immortal. Their abode was Mount Olympus and the airy regions above the earth.

Several religious or semi-religious ideas, which were a bequest to the Greeks from primitive times, and supplied them so often with motives of action, that we must not fail to take notice of them here. Two of these ideas related to the envious attitudes of the gods and the nature of life in the hereafter.

Their observation of life's experiences had taught them that continued good fortune and unusual prosperity often end in sudden and overwhelming calamity. They attributed this to the jealousy of the gods, who, they imagined were envious of mortals that through such prosperity seemed to have become too much like themselves.

To the Greeks, life here on earth was so bright and joyous a thing that they looked upon death as a great tragedy. Moreover, they pictured life after death, except in the case of a favored few, as being hopeless and aimless. The Elysian Fields, away in the land of sunset, were, indeed, filled with every delight; but these were the abode only of the great heroes and benefactors of the human race. The great mass of mankind was doomed to Hades, where the spirit existed as "a feeble, joyless phantom. " So long as the body remained unburied, the spirit wandered without rest; hence the extravagant funerals and expensive sepulchres of the ancient Greeks.

The Grecian influence may be considered a more lasting one than any of the ancient cultures, including even the Roman Empire. To this very day, world languages, social customs, and legal codes have strong and definite ancient Greek connections. When Alexander died, this dominating nation and culture was divided among his four generals:

(1) Cassander: Macedonia;

(2) Lysimachus: Asia Minor;
(3) Seleucus: Syria;
Ptolemy: Egypt.

This division is the prophecy in Daniel 11:4 which says, "... *his kingdom shall be broken, and shall be divided toward the four winds* ..."

But what about Daniel 11:5? First, read the verse carefully:

"And the king of the south shall be strung, and one of his princes; and he shall be strong above him, and have dominion; his dominion shall be a great dominion."

The king of the south was one of Alexander's generals. His name was Ptolemy I whose surname was Soter. He ruled in Egypt from 323 to 283 B.C. and seemed to possess much of his great commander's ability and restless energy, with a happy freedom from his worst faults.

Upon the partition of the empire of Alexander, Ptolemy had received Egypt, with parts of Arabia and Libya. To these he added by conquest Coele-Syria, Phoenicia, Palestine, Cyrene, and Cyprus. Following the custom of the time, he transported over one hundred thousand Jews from Jerusalem to Alexandria.

His aim was to make his capital city of Alexandria the intellectual center of the world—the place where the arts, sciences, literature, and religions of the world could meet and mingle. He founded a form of the modem college and established the renowned Alexandrian Library. He encouraged poets, artists, philosophers, and teachers in all departments of learning to settle in Alexandria by conferring upon them immunities and privileges, gifts and patronage.

Daniel 11:5 not only speaks of Ptolemy I, but it also speaks of .. *one of his princes.* .. "That prince was Seleucus Nicator who never matched in any discernible way the abilities and foresight of Ptolemy I. Very little is known of him except that he ruled an area from modem Israel to modem India.

Political marriages have always been an accepted institution among world leaders and their families in various nations. Daniel ll:6 tells of just such a marital alliance:

> "And in the end of years they shall join themselves together; for the king's daughter of the south shall come to the king of the north to make an agreement: but she shall not retain the power of the arm; neither shall he stand, nor his arm, but she shall be given up, and they that bought her, and he that begat her, and he that strengthened her in these times."

Here we have the account of the marriage of the daughter of Ptolemy II (28 3-247 B.C.) of Egypt to Antiochus I of Syria. Known also as Ptolemy Philadelphus, he followed closely in the footsteps of his father, carrying out as far as possible the plans and policies of the preceding reign. He added largely to the royal library, and he extended scholars the same liberal patronage that his father had given them. It was under his direction that the important Greek Translation of the old Hebrew Scriptures was begun. From the traditional number of translators (Latin septuaginta, "seventy") the version is known as the Septuagint.

The groom in this political marriage between Syria and Egypt was Antiochus I. His was not a noteworthy reign. Neither was his marriage. He left his bride after a brief and tumultuous relationship. His leadership of the nation of Syria ended with his assassination.

Daniel 1 1:7 is a reference to Ptolemy III, son of Ptolemy Philadelphus:

"But out of branch of her roots shall one stand up in his estate, which shall come with an army, and shall enter into the fortress of the king of the north, and shall deal against them, and shall prevail."

Partly because of revenge for the mistreatment of the Ptolemies by the Syrians during the above-mentioned marriage, and partly because of the fear of the increasing military build-up the Syrian army, Ptolemy III invaded the nation in 246 B C

From that point and for the next twenty-five years, a feud rages between the Ptolemies of Egypt and the Seleucidl of . Syria. Verses 8-13 speak of the back and forth conflicts. between them.

Antiochus III, also known as Antiochus the Great, ruled Syria from 192 to 189 B.C. His defeat of the Ptolemies and Egypt is the topic of Daniel 11:15-16:

"So the king of the north shall come, and cast up a mount, and take the most fenced cities: and the arms of the north shall not ' withstand, neither his chosen people, neither shall there be any strength to withstand. But he that cometh against him shall do according to his own will, and none shall stand before him: and he shall stand in the glorious land, which by his hand shall be consumed. "

To put it simply, Egypt was a pushover for the army I Antiochus the Great.

Having succeeded in defeating Egypt, Antiochus did an unusual thing. He ordered a marriage between his daughter and the deposed king of Egypt, Ptolemy V, thereby allowing him to keep his throne. Since I will not be sharing more of the history of Ptolemies, here is a side note. The last of the Ptolemies was the beautiful and deadly Cleopatra. In the year of 30 B.C,, which marks the year of her death, Egypt became a Roman province.

Daniel 1 1:18 details the continued exploits of Antiochus the Great: ,

After this shall he turn his face unto the isles, and shall take many: but a prince for his own behalf shall cause the reproach offered by him to cease; without his own reproach he shall cause it to turn upon him."

Antiochus made important conquests in Asia Minor and even ventured into Europe. He also entered Greece. The object of his presence in those regions, he declared, was to give liberty to the Greek cities. But the Greeks were at that particular time in no need of a liberator, since they had just been delivered from the Macedonians by the Romans.

Just as soon as intelligence was carried to Italy that the Syrian king was in Greece, at the head of an army, the armies of Greece were set in motion. Some reverses caused Antiochus to retreat in haste across the sea to Asia, followed hard by the Romans. At Magnesia, he was overthrown, and much of Asia Minor fell into the hands of the Romans.

Unable to accept his humiliation by the Romans, Antiochus the Great died, grieving himself to death:

"Then he shall turn his face toward the fort of his own land: but he shall stumble and fall, and not be found" (Daniel 11:19).

The son of Antiochus the Great was Seleueus IV. Also known as Philopator, he went back to the faltering kingdom of Syria, grimly waiting for an invasion by Rome that would finally destroy it completely. Making a last-ditch effort to revitalize his failing troops, he instituted a campaign appealing to the people's spirit of nationalism and patriotic pride. He tried to tax the people for sorely needed funds, but there was little response. Shortly therefore, realizing the certainty of the awful
inevitable, he took his own life:

"Then shall stand up in his estate a raiser of taxes in the glory of the kingdom: but within a few days he shall be destroyed, neither in anger, nor in battle" (Daniel 11:20).

Now we come to the man who pictures the antichrist who is yet to come during the seven years of tribulation. His name is Antiochus IV, or better known as Antiochus Epiphanes. This section about him in chapter eleven covers verses 21-35 and the final section of verses 36-45 is about the one he symbolizes, the dreaded antichrist.

Antiochus Epiphanes was a scheming and treacherous individual. Daniel 11:21 tells us that by political maneuvering and flattering words he was able to take the kingdom:

"And in his estate shall stand up a wide person, to whom they shall not give the honour of the kingdom: but he shall come in peaceably, and obtain the kingdom of flatteries. "

Get the perspective of the day! At the opening of the second century B.C., the Jews had been under the rule of the Seleucidae in Syria and surrounded by Greek influences for almost 150 years. During this period, the Greek customs had sunk deeply into the Jewish society. In Jerusalem, a great part of the Jews spoke

Greek, wore Greek clothes, and imitated the Greek way of life. Had this continued without interruption, the Jewish people might have become completely de-nationalized and the religious tradition upon which Christianity was built would have crumbled.

This threatened calamity was averted in the way that similar menacing calamities in the lives of races have been averted time and again in history--by a bad king. This was Antiochus IV (Epiphanes), who ruled from 176 to 164 B.C. Resolved upon the destruction of Judaism, he ordered all scrolls of the day destroyed, prohibited the Jewish worship and the observance of the Sabbath, and finally, set up a statue of Zeus Olympus on the great altar before the Temple in Jerusalem. In so doing, he substituted the worship of the Greek god for that of Jehovah. Those who refused to offer sacrifices on the pagan altars he put to death. Jerusalem was virtually transformed into a Greek colony. Never had the future of Israel been in more trouble than at this point in her history. A little more, and the Hebrew Bible would have been lost, and the Jewish religion would have been lost forever.

In Daniel 11:24-27, we have the account of Antiochus Epiphanes trying to establish diplomatic relationships with Egypt. Both the king of Egypt and Epiphanes were men of deception. They could not make peace treaties that were honored by both. Yet, they could not resolve their controversies decisively on the field of battle. It was upon returning from Egypt that Epiphanes began to vent his murderous and blasphemous attitudes against Israel:

"Then shall he return into his land with great riches: and his heart shall be against the holy covenant; and he shall do exploits, and return to his own land. . . and arms shall stand on his part. and they shall pollute the sanctuary of strength. And shall take away the daily sacrifice. and they shall place the abomination that maketh desolate" (l 1:28. 31).

You will note a reference in verse 30 to the ships of Chittim. Chittim is a term that is used to designate the early Roman state. Frightened by these military forces. Antiochus Epiphanes withdrew to Jerusalem even more than before and began a bloody massacre of those Jews who resisted him:

"And such as do wickedly against the co tenant shall he corrupt by flatteries: but the people that do know their God shall be strong, and do exploits. And they that understand among the people shall instruct many: yet they shall fall by the sword. And by flame, by captivity, and by spoil, many days" (Daniel l 1:32-33).

As mentioned earlier in the study of this chapter, the remaining verses (36~45) refer to the antichrist who is yet to make his appearance on the world scene:

"And the king shall do according to his will; and he shall exalt himself and magnify himself above every god, and shall speak marvelous things against the God of gods. and shall prosper till the indignation be accomplished: for that which is determined shall be done. Neither shall he regard the God of his fathers, nor the desire of women, nor regard any god: for he shall magnify himself above all" (Daniel l 1:36-37).

These verses tell us several things that we may use as identifying marks of the antichrist:

(l) HE WILL MAGNIFY HIMSELF;
(2) HE WILL BLASPI-IEME GOD: '
(3) HE WILL TEMPORARILY PROSPER;
(4) 1112 WILL REFUSE ms RELIGIOUS UPBRINGING;
(5) HE WILL REJECT WOMANI-IOOD;
(6) HE WILL ACTUALLY BE NON-RELIGIOUS.

We also are told something very important about the antichrist in verse 38:

"But in his estate shall he honor the god of forces and a god whom his fathers knew not shall he honor with gold. and silver; and precious stones, and pleasant things "

The gods of the antichrist, according to this verse, will be the gods of:

(I) MONEY;

(2) MILITARY.

The remaining verses show the antichrist as he will one day jockey for political and military advantage. Caught between the thrusts of Egypt from the south and Syria from the north, but the antichrist will emerge in victory. Returning to Jerusalem, he will establish his headquarters, but his final destruction is predicted in verse 45:

. . yet he shall come to his end, and none shall help him. "

Also, in Revelation 19:11-21 can be found a complete description of the Battle of Armageddon where the antichrist, also called "the beast. " will meet his defeat at the hands of Jesus. Look at verses 19 and 20:

"And I saw the beast, and the kings of the earth. and their armies, gathered together to make war against him that sat on the horse, and against his army. And the beast was taken, and with him the false prophet that wrought miracles before hint. with which he deceived them that had received the mark of the beast, and them that worshipped his image. These both were cast alive into a lake burning with fire and brimstone. "

Chapter Twelve

The Two Resurrections

We have now come to the concluding chapter of the Book of Daniel. The towering pinnacles of prophetic truths have been ours to behold. The human interest stories of good men and wicked tyrants have been embellishments for this intriguing narrative of the unfolding plan of the ages. But now we will hear the final remarks by Daniel, one of history's most remarkable men.

Anytime we come to the end of things, whether it is the end of a sporting event or the end of a course of study or the sobering end of life itself, we become acutely aware of time. Please note how often "*times* " is used in verse one:

"And at that TIME shall Michael stand up, the great prince who standeth for the children of thy people, and there shall be a TIME of trouble, such as never was since there was a nation even to that same TIME; and at that TIME thy people shall be delivered, every one that shall be found written in the book."

Such emphasis by the recurring reminders of time is to burn in our minds the certainty of God's control of passing events as they flow toward specific and fixed divine appointments. God is sovereign in power and omniscient in knowledge. There are no conjectures, happen-stances, or accidents in the plans of the Almighty. Times are set! Times are established! Dear Reader, as you have inched along through this study, has it not brought a sense of assurance to recognize the preciseness of the timing of events by our Lord? We can take great comfort indeed that the eventualities of our lives are point-by-point in accordance with God's predetermined calendar of eternity.

Verse one begins with the coordinating conjunction "*and,* " which ties chapter 12 to chapter 11. As we have already observed, chapter 11 is a discussion of the end time as it pertains to the antichrist. Chapter 12 is also a discussion of the end-time, but this material revolves around the Lord Jesus Christ.

Introduced immediately to us is Michael, an angel of the Most High god. He is of high rank, is described in the Scriptures in his role as guardian and protector of Israel, and is fully aware of the limitations of power in struggles against Satan. That recognition of the boundaries of his strength and the position of his strength and the position of his direct involvement with important matters relating to Israel is seen in Jude:

"Yet Michael, the archangel, when contending with the devil he disputed about the body of Moses, durst not bring against him a railing accusation, but said, the Lord rebuke thee "(verse 9).

Again, in Revelation 12:7, Michael can be seen at war with the devil and his angels in a chapter that is centered around the nation of Israel:

"And there was war in heaven; Michael and his angels fought against the dragon, and the dragon fought and his angels. "

Returning to Daniel 12:1, we have a further confirmation of Michael's role as a defender of Israel with this phrase, ". . . *The great prince who standeth for the children of thy people. . .* " For those who know God and the teachings of His Word, there is no mystery about Israel's uncanny ability to withstand enormous military aggression in our day. The tiny nation has an angel as its principal weapon of defense. Nuclear weapons, rockets, and jet fighters are no matter for the arm of Michael, the angel of God!

But after all, does it not seem reasonable that a nation chosen of God would have divine assistance to the challenges of its very existence? Verse one clearly identifies Israel with the phrase, *. . the children of thy peo*ple . . . " God loves this little nation! And whether the fact of His love for them conforms to personal ideologies or political postures by the governmental leaders of other countries, it is nevertheless an unequivocal scriptural fact that the entire socio-economic system of the world revolves around this little Middle East nation.

I am an American. My heart still flutters a bit when Old Glory is carried past me on parade. I have no respect for those who trample it under foot, burn their draft cards, or shout obscenities at the President of the United States who may be either Democrat or Republican. As much as I love my two sons, I would not want them to refuse drafting into our armed services in defense of our great country against any other nation on this earth-with the exception of Israel. I feel an uneasiness creep over me when I hear our leaders in foreign policy talk about enacting procedures that would adversely affect the Jew. Why do I have that feeling? God told Abraham in the twelfth chapter of Genesis that he would be very mindful of the attitudes of other nations toward His nation:

"And I will bless them that bless thee. and curse him that curseth thee; and in thee shall all families of the earth be blessed " (Genesis 12:3).

It is my conviction that one of the foremost reasons for the unprecedented and continued prosperity of the United States lies in the support that we have always given Israel. We have been the beneficiaries of the promise made in the verse just quoted. Other countries have injected themselves with a fatal dose of political poison that resulted in their own national destruction when they presumptuously moved against the Jew.

In A.D. 70, Titus Audronicus surrounded Jerusalem with his iron legions of Rome. The abdomens of pregnant women were cruelly ripped open. Mass starvation from their siege forced many of the Jews into cannibalism. The mountains around Jerusalem were covered with crosses upon which were hundreds of Jews crucified. But God did not forget! The deadening decay of Rome's impending doom was set in motion on that fateful day.

We could outline the atrocities perpetrated by the Turks. We might consider the awful holocaust in Germany under Hitler in this century during which six million Jews met untimely deaths. Both of these nations, and others that might be named, fell from lofty heights when they disturbed the *"apple of God's eye. "*

The most graphic example of God's protective care in thwarting the plans of those who would destroy Israel is yet to occur but is presented in detail in the thirty-eighth chapter of Ezekiel. The entire chapter describes the future invasion of the Holy Land by the U.S.S.R. and certain other countries who will join in the attack. It is not necessary to this study of the Book of Daniel for us to study Ezekiel 38 in detail, but because of the significance of the battle we must look briefly to a few of the verses that highlight the battle.

Blazing daily in our newspapers are stories of the massive Russian arms build-up and the questions of whether the nuclear capabilities of the U.S.S.R. are greater than those of the United States. Accompanying these reports are often accounts of the plight of the Jews in the Soviet Union and their generally futile efforts to leave. This powerhouse north of the Holy Land struts its atheism in the arena of international human rights. Because they are so anti-God and the Jew is so pro-God, they are natural enemies. And, for that reason, Russia hates Israel.

Lest you think that l am guilty of reading too much into the Scriptures, please read Ezekiel 38:1-2:

"And the word of the Lord came unto me, saying. Son of man, set thy face against Gog of the land of Magog, the chief prince of Meshech and Tubal. "

"Gog" is the ancient name for the Ukrainian region in southern Russia. During World War II there wooden pencils manufactured in the Ukraine with the inscription on the side, *"Made In The Land Of Gog. "* The title, *"chief prince*, "is the word, '*Rash*, " from "*rucia*, " in the original language, and it is the word from which we get the word, "*Russia*."

"*Meshech*" is an interesting word. When doing undergraduate work in a secular university, I elected to take three quarters of Russian history. This apparent choice made by me alone was actually made by God, and the knowledge I gleaned in those studies have proven invaluable in the study of God's Word. One of the things I learned was that Meshech is the original name for the capital city of the U.S.S.R., Moscow. Another word you see in Ezekiel 38:1 is "*Tubal*. " If you add the common Russian suffix, "*sk*", you now have "*Tubalsk*, " the older way of rendering a Siberian area in present-day Russian, "Tobolsk." Another scriptural evidence that this future enemy of Israel is the U.S.S.R. can be found in Ezekiel 38: 15:

"And thou shalt come from thy place out of the north parts . . . "

If you should take a map and draw a line due north from Jerusalem, you would go right through Moscow. This is one of the most exciting chapters, and also one of the most detailed in prophetic statements, that can be found in the Word of God. I recommend that you study it thoroughly. The climax of God's wrath upon these haters of Israel is proclaimed in Ezekiel 39:1-4, 12:

"Therefore, thou son of man, prophecy against Gog. and say, Thus saith

the Lord God, Behold I am against thee, 0 God, the chief prince of Meshech and Tubal, and I will turn thee back, and leave but the sixth part of thee. and will cause thee to come up from the north parts, and will bring thee upon the mountains of Israel. And I will smite thy bow out of thy right hand. . . Thou shalt fall upon the mountains of Israel, thou and all thy bands, and the peoples that are with thee; I will give thee unto the ravenous birds of every sort, and to the beasts of the field to be devoured . . . so will I make my holy name known in the midst of my people Israel, and I will not let them pollute my holy name any more; and the heathen shall know that I am the Lord, the Holy One in Israel. . . and seven months shall the house of Israel be burying them, that they may cleanse the land. "

Can you imagine the devastation that is foretold in these verses. The conquest of the Soviet army will be so complete that only one-sixth of the troops will be able to stagger from the battlefields. So many will die that the Jews will spend seven months burying the slain soldiers of mighty Russia. The U.S.S.R. is a doomed nation, with no hope at all when they finally come down to attack little Israel.

But the most important phrase in Daniel 12:1 is, *. . And there shall be a time of trouble . . .*" This expression is just another way of describing the seven years of great tribulation which are yet to come. We have already discussed the seventy weeks of Daniel found in chapter nine. You will recall that God plans to lift the partial spiritual blindness from the eyes of national Israel after the removal of the church at the rapture, and He plans to develop them as His people in the Holy Land during the tribulation.

This clear Biblical teaching has been the object of the liberal's scorn for centuries. They scoffed at the notion that God had a plan for Israel. After all, they reasoned, Israel as a nation did not even exist. It had fallen prey to the sword of ancient Babylon over five hundred years before Christ. Any student of sociology knows that such displaced peoples who are removed from their homeland lose their national identity, their cultural heritage, their ability to speak their native tongue, and are never able to re-establish themselves as a nation. But after 2500 years the impossible actually occurred, for in May of 1948, the modern state of Israel was born! God's miracle promise of re-gathering in Isaiah 11:11-12 had been fulfilled:

"And it shall come to pass in that day, that the Lord' shall set his hand again the second time to recover the remnant of his people, who shall be left, from Assyria, and from Egypt, and from Pathros, and from Cush, and from Elam. and from Shinar, and from Hamath, and from the islands of the sea. And he shall set up an ensign for the nations, and shall assemble the outcasts of Israel. and gather together the dispersed of Judah front the four corners of the earth."

One objection often raised is that there is just as much reason to believe that this passage is in reference to Israel's release from Babylonian captivity as it is in reference to the end of time. However, there are two good reasons that we can positively know that these verses are a prophetic statement of events yet to occur. First, when the Jews left Babylon, there were not other Jews who joined them in rebuilding Jerusalem who had been residing in Assyria, Egypt, Pathros, Cush, Hamath, or the islands. Historically, either in the Bible or in the secular record, there can be found no accounts at all of this prophecy having been fulfilled, Second, please note the phrase, *. . and gather together the dispersed of Judah from the four comers of the earth."* It has only been within the last four hundred years that the Jews have been scattered to the four corners" of the earth. Since, therefore, the regathering of the Jews of global dimensions has not yet occurred, we must conclude that the event is a future one.

However, we are, in these present days, seeing that regathering gaining momentum as thousands upon thousands of people of Jewish heritage are going back to the land of their fathers. Sometimes they cannot even logically explain why they have decided to leave secure roots and go to a land of insecurity and danger. On one of my recent visits to Israel, it was my privilege to make the acquaintance of a young medical doctor from Brooklyn, New York who left his practice, moved to Israel and subsequently lost a leg as an infantryman serving in the Israeli army during the Six Days War in 1967. When I asked him why he left a lucrative medical practice in the United States to come to an impoverished and war-ridden land, he replied that he really could not explain his choice other than the fact that he just simply developed an overwhelming desire to move to the Holy Land. I believe that that desire was the homing signal of the Holy Spirit as God had started bringing His people home again.

To the casual observer of Jewish current events, there seems to be an emerging exodus from Israel that has been shaping for the last few years;

therefore, the conclusion could be reached that a re-gathering is not actually taking place. In response, it must be pointed out that there are more Jews entering Palestine than are leaving it. Indeed. the reality is obvious that for the first time in 2500 years, the Jews possess their ancient land of the Abrahamic promise and this one statement contemporary truths places them in a perfect position for the beginning of the *"time of trouble"* or *"the great tribulation. "*

That future time will be unbelievably horrible. Jeremiah was well aware of the agony of those days and prophesied:

"And these are the words that the Lord spoke concerning Israel and concerning Judah. For thus saith the Lord, we have heard a voice of trembling, of fear, and not of peace. Ask now, and see whether a man doth travail with child? Wherefore do I see every man with his hands on his loins, like a woman in travail, and all faces are turned into paleness? Alas, for that day is great, so that none is like it; it is even the time of Jacob's trouble, but he shall be saved out of it " (Jeremiah 30:4-7).

Pain will be so great in those days that men will be seen holding themselves in discomfort like pregnant women.

Perhaps the best reason for the great tribulation that can be found in the Old Testament is found in Ezekiel 20:33-38:

"As I live, saith the Lord God, surely with a mighty hand, and with a stretched out arm, and with fury poured out, will I rule over you. And I will bring you out from the peoples, and will gather you out of the countries in which ye are scattered, with a mighty hand, and with a stretched out arm, and with fury poured out. And I will bring you into the wilderness of the peoples, and there will I plead with you, saith the Lord God. and I will cause you to pass under the rod, and I will bring you into the bond of the covenant. And I will purge out from among you the rebels, and them that transgress against me; I will bring them forth out of the country where they sojourn, and they shall not enter into the land of Israel; and ye shall know that I am the Lord. "

Let us now return to Daniel 12:2 which shows the exciting Bible doctrine of two eternal judgments. Do not be misled by those who teach a general judgment where lost men and saved men are separated one from the other. There is no scriptural support for a general judgment. What the Bible teaches is a doctrine of two resurrections and two judgments. Here, in Daniel 12:2 we have this phrase which pertains to the saved:

"And many of them that sleep in the dust of the earth shall awake, some to everlasting life . .

Compare this with Revelation 20:6:

"Blessed and holy is he that hath part in the first resurrection: on such the second death hath no power, but they shall be priests of God and of Christ. and shall reign with him a thousand years. "

This first resurrection of the saved is the next scheduled event on God's great prophetic timetable. As you already know, we call it the rapture of the church. Immediately following the rapture will be the judgment seat of Christ. Only the saved will be present:

"Now if any man build upon this foundation gold. silver. precious stones, wood, hay, stubble; every man's work shall be made manifest for the day shall declare it, because it shall be revealed by fire: and the,/ire shall try every man's work of what sort it is. If any man's work abide, which he hath built thereupon, he shall receive a reward. If any man's work shall be burned, he shall suffer loss: but he himself shall be saved; yet so as by fire" (I Corinthians 3:12-15).

The second part of Daniel 12:2 is a reference to the resurrection of the unsaved who must then stand before the great white throne judgment. Daniel 12:2 states:

". . . and some to shame and everlasting contempt."

Oh, Dear Reader, how sad will be that awful day of judgment when lost men, women, boys, and girls are brought from the grave to stand before God. Revelation 20:11-15 tells of that unspeakable horror.

"And I saw a great white throne, and him that sat on it, from whose face

the earth and the heaven fled away, and there was found no place for them. And I saw the dead, small and great, stand before God, and the books were opened; and another book was opened, which is the book of life. And the dead were judged out of those things which were written in the books, according to their works. And the sea gave up the dead which were in it, and death and hell delivered up the dead which were in them; and they were judged every man according to their works. And death and hell were cast into the lake of fire. This is the second death. And whosoever was not found written in the book of life was cast into the lake of fire. "

From these verses we learn that men will be judged from material that is recorded in three books:

(1) BOOK OF LIFE'S ACTIVITIES: Every deed done during the years that God gives a man upon earth will come under divine scrutiny:

"For we must all appear before the judgment sat of Christ; that everyone may receive the things done in his body, according to that he hath done, whether it be good or bad" (II Corinthians 5:10).

"For shall bring every work into judgment, with every secret thing, whether it be good, or whether it be evil" (Ecclesiastes 12:14).

God is keeping a daily record of every man's life. Please remember! The Great White Throne Judgment of the unsaved will not provide an opportunity for men to be saved. This judgment, like the judgment of the saved that takes place after the rapture, is solely a judgment of works. A man will suffer in hell in direct proportion to his sins while on earth. Does this mean that the flames of hell will be hotter for some who go there than others? Of course not! Please look at Revelation 22:11:

"He that is unjust, let him be unjust still, and he that is filthy, let him be filthy still; and he that is righteous, let him be righteous still, and he that is holy, let him be holy still. "

In other words, if a man is an alcoholic, he will be an alcoholic for an eternity in hell but with no way to quench his alcoholic thirst. If a man is sexually perverted, he will be obsessed with illicit desires for an eternity in hell but with no way to satisfy his lusts. If a man is addicted to drugs, he will live with eternal withdrawal pains in hell but with no way to ease the torment. Whatever sins a man allows in this world to stand between him and his acceptance of Jesus will be his for eternity to remind him of his foolishness.

(2) BOOK OF GOD'S WORDS: The Lord has given us sixty-six books in one magnificent book that we call the Holy Bible. These words will be used as the basis of judgment. See John 12:47-50:

"And if any man hear my words, and believe not, I judge him not, for I come, not to judge the world but to save the world. He that rejecteth me, and receiveth not my words, hath one that judgeth him: the word that I have spoken, the same shall judge him in the last day. For I have not spoken of myself: but the Father; who sent me, he gave me a commandment, what I should say, and what I should speak. And I know that his commandment is life everlasting; whatsoever I speak, therefore, even as the Father said unto me. so I speak."

The best reason that I can give you for studying carefully the Word of God is given in these verses. We will be judged by the commandments and principles shared in the Scriptures.

(3) BOOK OF LIFE: The Lamb's Book of Life has the names of all who are to be in heaven recorded on its pages. A misconception about this book is that a name is added when that particular person is saved. That is incorrect. Actually, the
Book of Life initially had the name of every person who was ever born physically into this world. When a person rejects Christ's salvation for the final time, his name is blotted out. It is eternally removed! Proof of this erasure is found in Exodus 32:32-33:

"Yet now, if thou will forgive their sin—; and if not, blot me, I pray thee, out of thy book which thou hast written. And the Lord said unto Moses, Whosoever hath sinned against me, him will I blot out of my book."

This book is the supreme record of the ages! Be sure that you are saved! Do not be blotted out!

Revelation 20:13 gives us an interesting and frequently unseen truth. The Bible says that "*death and hell delivered up the dead that were in them.* " When a lost man dies, his body is placed in the grave, and his soul is placed in hell. Here, in this verse, the residing place of the body is "*death*." The word, "*hell*, " as used here, is actually "*hades*, " a "*holding place.* " When the Great White Throne Judgment is called, God will reach into the grave for the body of the lost man and simultaneously reach into hades for the soul of the lost man. He will reunite soul and body for an appearance before the throne. Remember the words of Jesus in Matthew 10:28:

"And fear not them who kill the body, but are not able to kill the soul; but rather fear him who is able to destroy both soul and body in hell. "

Revelation 20:14 shows that God will cast both soul and body into the lake of fire after the judgment. Do not allow yourself the luxury of thinking or presuming at all that a lost man has a second chance after death. He does not! If he is not saved when he draws his final breath, he never will be!

Why is this banishment in the lake of fire called the "second death " in Revelation 20:14? Is it really death into an unconscious state of nonexistence in annihilation as some suggest? It is called the second death because the first death is obviously the physical one that precedes it. It is called "*death* " because it is separation from God to enter a state of sheer hopelessness. It does not at all mean unconsciousness. Sadly, but in divine justice, a man will be fully aware and sensitive to all the pains of hell for all eternity.

Perhaps it seems to you that I have given undue or excess consideration to the first two verses of chapter twelve of Daniel. But the vital importance of the message contained in them cannot be overestimated. On the backdrop of those words, we arrive now to Daniel 12:3 and its wondrous declaration:

"And they that be wise shall shine as the brightness of the firmament; and they that turn many to righteousness as the stars forever and ever." '

True scriptural wisdom is really the only kind that exists. The world wrongly defines "*wisdom* " as "*common sense* "; but it is actually "*uncommon sense.* " It is a supernatural quality that is given to the seeking believer: "H any of you lack wisdom, let him ask of God, that giveth to all men liberally, and upbraideth not: and it shall be given him" (James 1:5).

Dear Reader, please know that wisdom has not the remotest attachment to formed learning. The poorest of men and the most unlearned of the unlearned can be rich in this divine spiritual trait. How so? I see that wisdom is not at all a grace gift such as those listed for us in the twelfth chapter of 1 Corinthians and the twelfth chapter of Romans. Those gifts are sovereignly bestowed upon whomsoever the Lord may select without works of achievement by the believers. wisdom, however, is in contrast to such grace gifts in that it is within reach of any believer who will consider two requirements:

(1) He must ask God for wisdom as already indicated in James 1:5;
(2) He must *"turn many to righteousness"* (Daniel 12:3).

By praying to God and proclaiming the gospel a man is viewed by the Lord as "wise" and how desperately our world needs "*wise men!*"

Just because the scientific and technological communities are mushrooming with ever accelerating speeds, we are still no more exempted from the basic problems of sin, sorrow, and death than were our forefathers of the ancient past. We may wear business suits instead of loin cloths, we may ride in jet planes instead of on donkey backs, but we continue to live, grow old, and die in our individual patterns of continual difficulties and painful situations. It is little wonder that the couch of the psychiatrist is becoming a status symbol of our age. Modem man is craving for a word from his god just as Amos had predicted long ago:

"Behold, the days come, saith the Lord God, that I will send a famine in the land, not a famine of bread, nor of thirst for water, but of hearing the words of the Lord: and they shall wander from sea to sea, and from the north even to the east, they shall run to and fro to seek the Word of the Lord, and shall not find it" (Amos 8:11-12).

It is to that very need that the cross of Christ must be preached. We must never allow ourselves to parade the cross of Jesus upon the shoulders of the world's liberal ideas of what Christianity ought to be. This world system of religion preaches that we are made right with God through the humanitarian good deeds that we do for our fellow man. That is worldly wisdom; we must not be intimidated by it. Charitable acts do not result in salvation; they are the result of salvation. A lengthy, but applicable, statement is made by Paul in the first chapter of the first Corinthian letter in which he pointedly contrasts wisdom of the world and the wisdom of the Lord:

"For Christ sent me not to baptize, but to preach the gospel, not with WISDOM of words, lest the cross of Christ should be made of none effect. F or the preaching of the cross is to them that perish, foolishness; but unto us which are saved it is the power of God. For it is written, I will destroy the WISDOM of the wise and will bring to nothing the understanding of the prudent. Where is the wise? Where is the scribe? Where is the disputer of this world? Hath not God made foolish the WISDOM of this world? For alter that in the WISDOM of God the world by WISDOM knew not God, it pleased God by the foolishness of preaching to save them that believe. For the Jews require a sign, and the Greeks seek after WISDOM. But we preach Christ crucified, unto the Jews a stumbling block, and unto the Greeks foolishness; but unto them which are called, both Jews and Greeks, Christ the power of God, and the WISDOM of God. Because the foolishness of God is wiser than men; and the weakness of God is stronger than men. For ye see your calling, brethren, how that not many wise men alter The flesh, not many mighty, not many noble, are called but God hath chosen the foolish things of the world to confound the wise; and God hath chosen the weak things of the world to confound the things that are mighty; and base things of the world, and things which are despised, hath God chosen, yea, and things which are not, to bring to naught, things that are, that no flesh should glory in his presence. But of him are ye in Christ Jesus, who of God is made unto us WISDOM, and righteousness, and sanctification, and redemption; that, according as it is written, he that glorieth, let him glory in the Lord" (verses 17:31).

I realize that this constitutes a rather lengthy segment of quoted material from the Scriptures, but it very graphically, very explicitly, details the differences between the wisdom of God and the wisdom of man. Let the world honor its "stars" with medals, ribbons, and statuettes, God rewards His "stars" with eternal illumination in the light of His own blessed presence. No higher more prestigious title can be attached to an individual's name than that of soulwinner.

Beginning in Daniel 12:4 we are given the final message of the Lord to the prophet Daniel. This remarkable prophecy is for the "... *time of the end* .. Make no mistake of interpretation! This little phrase cannot be ignored; neither can it be assigned in reference to any previous time period in the history of our world. In fact, the phrase is unquestionably a reference to the seven years of the tribulation period.

How can we know that? First, as we have already observed in this study, the great tribulation period is a priority subject in the Book of Daniel. Second. please note the words tucked in chapter twelve, verse seven, .. *that it shall be for a time, times, and a half.* . Ordinarily, this phrase is used as another way of stating three and one-half years. For example, in Revelation 12:14, this exact same phrase, .. time, and times, and half a time. . . "is included in connection with the tribulation. For these two reasons, we can know that Daniel's twelfth chapter is yet to be fulfilled.

As a general predition, verse four places this prophecy in the end-time by saying, .. *many shall run to and fro, and knowledge shall be increased.*" We are already being participants in these two observations. Ours is the most mobile society in history with approximately 1 out of 10 families in America making a residential move every twelve months. The common complaint of our contemporary lifestyles is that everything is moving too fast. And never has our world been so full in its head and empty in its heart. Knowledge is increasing at such rapid rates that we presently have more scientists alive today than have ever lived.

In verse five, the vision begins. He sees a river. On either side of that river can be seen two men. Above the river is a third man. That third man is a theophany of the Lord Jesus Christ. We have already in this study acquainted ourselves with theophanies when we looked into the fiery furnace and saw the Son of God standing with Shadrach, Meshach and Abednego. Remember that a theophany is an Old Testament appearance of Jesus. Therefore, the man above the river is Jesus.

This revelation of the Son of God to Daniel must have gladdened the heart of the old prophet. In verse four he had just been instructed to .. *shut up and seal the book even to the time of the end* . . . " How strange this mysterious command had been to the ears of this man of God! But now, looking up into the face of Jesus, it was all made clear. God was making provisions for the people who would be living during the end-time and particularly for the world's inhabitants at the time of the tribulation. Even those of us in this present age may take comfort as recipients of Christ's command that resulted in the preservation of the prophecies of Daniel and their safe passage down to us through the many intervening years.

One of the men at the river in Daniel's vision asked a question that was probably also lodged in the prophet's own heart, . . how long shall it be to the end of these wonders?" (verse 6). The answer comes immediately from the lips of Christ in verse seven as He pinpoints the last three and one-half years of the tribulation with His reference to ". . . time, times, and an half. . ." But even greater clarity of the period in question is given when our Lord declares that . . he shall have accomplished to scatter the power of the body of the holy people, all these things shall be finished " (verse 7). Luke, in the New Testament, speaks of the same time frame by saying:

"And they shall fall by the sword, and shall be led away captive into all nations; and Jerusalem shall be trodden down by the Gentiles, until the times of the Gentiles be fulfilled. And there shall be signs in the sun, and in the moon, and in the stars; and upon the earth distress of nations, with perplexity; the sea and the waves roaring. Men 's hearts failing them for fear, and for looking after those things which are coming on the earth; for the powers of heaven shall be shaken. And then shall they see the Son of man coming in a cloud, with power and great glory. And when these things begin to come to pass, then look up, and lift up your heads; for your redemption draweth nigh" (Luke 21:24-28).

Perhaps Daniel stood for a moment silently trying to comprehend the words of the Lord. Finally, in what seems to be an almost under the breath comment, he says, "*and I heard, but I understood not. . .* "(verse 8). I am so glad for that verse! Even this grand old man of God, to whom so much of God's mind had been revealed, did not understand everything said by the Lord. That gives me such comfort as I face impenetrable truths in God's Word, not at all the product of human ingenuity.

But a promise is shared in verse 10 that although the days of judgment

will eventually come and men's hearts will continue to grow increasingly perverse, those who are saved "... *shall understand.* " Paul expresses the same thoughts in
I Corinthians 2:14:

> *"But the natural man receiveth not the things of the Spirit of God; for they are foolishness unto him, neither can he know them, for they are spiritually discerned. "*

We now come to the final three verses of Daniel: These verses are some of the most difficult in the entire Bible to interpret. We do know that the .. abomination that maketh desolate . . ." (verse 11) is a phrase that has previously been used in Daniel 9:27 and later by Jews in Matthew 24:15 to describe the mid-point of the seven-year tribulation week.

But why does Daniel speak of .. *a thousand two hundred and ninety days?*" (verse 11). Three and one-half years is forty-two months or a thousand two hundred and sixty days. Here, in Daniel 12:11, however, there seems to be a problem by the presence of an additional thirty days or one prophetic month in his prophecy. While this isolated and unique statement has been variously interpreted, it is my considered opinion that this thirty-day period will provide adequate time for the judgment of the Gentiles in an examination of their treatment of the Jews during the tribulation (Matthew 25).

Daniel 12:12 uses another unusual number of a .. *Thousand three hundred and five and thirty days.* " This gives us an additional seventy-five days beyond the end of the tribulation period. We might summarize the-days in this fashion. At the mid-point of the tribulation will occur the abomination of desolations. Then, twelve hundred and sixty days (3½ years) will bring us to the end of the tribulation week marked by the Battle of Armageddon. Next, the thirty days of Gentile judgment appear. Finally, another forty-five days will bring the saints (note "blessed" in verse 12) to the inauguration of Christ' millennial kingdom.

The final verse in the Book of Daniel provides him, and us, with a wondrous promise: .. *thou shalt rest, and stand in thy lot at the end of days.* " In other words, Daniel is told that although he must die, he will enjoy a future resurrection from the dead. God never forgets His people!

      I have been personally blessed and inspired to do more for our dear Lord as I have prepared these study chapters for you. It is my prayer that because you have labored through these pages that the urgency of the hour will be pressed upon your heart. If so, it will have made my efforts in this book a gain and not a loss for the kingdom's sake.

www.ingramcontent.com/pod-product-compliance
Lightning Source LLC
Chambersburg PA
CBHW050906160426
43194CB00011B/2305